The Code Cannot be Broken

A Key to Spiritual Revelation and Power with God

CHRISTINA BURKE

WESTBOW°
PRESS
A DIVISION OF THOMAS NELSON
& ZONDERVAN

WestBow Press books may be ordered through booksellers or by contacting:

WestBow Press
A Division of Thomas Nelson & Zondervan
1663 Liberty Drive
Bloomington, IN 47403
www.westbowpress.com
1 (866) 928-1240

ISBN: 978-1-4908-7757-0 (sc)

Library of Congress Control Number: 2015906265

Print information available on the last page.

WestBow Press rev. date: 07/08/2015

Contents

Special Thanks

I would like to give thanks to my Lord and Savior for the opportunity to write this book. Also, my heart felt appreciation to my husband Rick who made time to edit the book and for his patience with me during this time. Last, but certainly not least, thanks to Nancy Tharp for assisting with the finishing touches.

Dedication

I take pleasure in dedicating this book "The Code Cannot Be Broken" to my beloved dad Nelson Draper Sr., my uncle Teddy Draper Sr. and all other Navajo Code Talkers.

Thank you for your willingness to obey our Creator in fighting for our nation.

Semper Fidelis!
Always faithful, Always loyal!

I give honor where honor is due

God had a plan from the very beginning and it was accomplished.

In love,
Christina Burke

Introduction

IN THE BEGINNING

*"In the beginning was the Word, and the Word was with
God, and the Word was God. He was in the beginning
with God. All things were made. Through Him, and
without Him nothing was made that was made."*

—*John 1:1–3*

During WWII in the Pacific theater, the US military
command sought an efficient, undecipherable code to be used
for the communication of tactical information. The Navajo
language was considered to answer those requirements. It was
spoken only in the region of the Navajo reservation in the
American Southwest. The complexity of the language made it
unintelligible to anyone without extensive training or exposure
to it. It was largely an unwritten language at that time. One
estimation asserted that fewer than thirty non-Navajos in the
world could understand the language.

The US Marine Corps recruited more than four hundred
young Navajo men to become Code Talkers. Their primary
job was to send and receive transmissions of secret tactical
messages using communications nets. They developed formal

and informal codes built upon their native language. The speed and accuracy with which messages were sent and received was unmatched by any other means of communication.

At the Battle of Iwo Jima, a signal officer from the 5th Marine Division, Major Howard Connor, had six Navajo Code Talkers under his command working around the clock. These men transmitted and received more than eight hundred messages without error. Major Connor later noted that had it not been for the Navajos the Marines would never have taken Iwo Jima.

Though the eavesdropping Japanese were masterful code breakers, the Navajo code sounded like nothing more than gibberish to them. They remained perplexed by the Navajo language. The Japanese Chief of Intelligence, Lieutenant General Seizo Arisue, said that although they deciphered the codes used by the US Army and the Army Air Corps, they never cracked the code used by the Marines. Consequently, the enemy was never able to use the communicated battle plans that they intercepted.

The vital role of young Navajo Marines and the code they used so effectively was instrumental in expediting the ultimate victory for America and her allies. The Code Talkers are credited with significant contributions to the American victories on Guadalcanal, Iwo Jima, and other major battles in the islands of the Pacific. Consequently, the lives of untold numbers of American soldiers were saved.

Even after the war ended, the Navajo code remained classified as "secret." No recognition of note was given to the Navajo Marines who demonstrated such courageous patriotism until years later, when the code was declassified by the Department of Defense in 1968. After fifty-six years, in July and November of 2001, Navajo Code Talkers were awarded

Congressional Gold Medals and Congressional Silver Medals respectively.

America's victory in the Pacific theater is one example among many in American history in which the sovereign hand of God intervened with divine protection and favor in a time of conflict for the sake of a people who would pray fervently and seek Him.

God knows "the end from the beginning."[1] God did, in fact, have a preordained plan for communicating with His greatest and most wonderful creation, man. He has made a way for every Christian believer individually and also for His corporate body, the church, to connect with Him, spirit to Spirit. This communication is a heavenly code that cannot be deciphered by any enemy of God or man. It is spoken to the hidden man of the spirit by the Holy Spirit of God.

In the book of Acts we read about the enabling provision of the early church that empowered it to function in divine ability.

> *"They were all with one accord in one place. And suddenly there came a sound from heaven, as of a rushing mighty wind, and it filled the whole house where they were sitting. Then there appeared to them divided tongues, as of fire, and one sat upon each of them. And they were all filled with the Holy Spirit and began to speak with other tongues, as the Spirit gave them utterance."*
>
> *—Acts 2:1–4*

By this heavenly code, God transmits His power, His wisdom, and His glory into and through His church.

---

[1] Isaiah 46:10

Understanding of divine principles, strategies, and instructions formerly mysterious and unknowable, by natural means, are now revealed by the Holy Spirit in those who are submitted to and are in His love.[2] The goal of this all-inclusive plan for the one true church is to cause His undivided kingdom to be made manifest in the earth. This is available to all who would align themselves with His heart and His Word.[3]

The church is given this powerful weapon to coordinate not only battle plans but also divine plans and strategies that have been preordained from the beginning of time. This "sound" first uttered by believers at the birth of the true Christian church was a heavenly communication of the Holy Spirit. This mighty sound intimidates the enemy. When the people of God hear, obey, and carry out the plans and strategies of God, they always frustrate those of the devil. He is the enemy of God and of every man.

The Navajo Code Talkers rallied together in one accord, in agreement, with one mission and one goal. What only they had the ability to do was key to the winning of not just one battle, but rather, of the entire war in the Pacific.

God is rallying His people today with this same focus and equipping them to bring about the ultimate end of demonic hostilities on the earth.

The concerted practice of this wonderful language code is key to bringing about unity of soul and spirit within each believer and, consequently, outward in the Body of Christ. The harmony of agreement brought about by the union of the natural mind (renewed by the Word of God) and the abiding leadership of the Holy Spirit within results in the singleness of heart and purpose—i.e., of Christ. This leads to action.

---

[2] 1 Corinthians 2:9–10

[3] Romans 10:13, Ephesians 4:4–6

Those who believe and are able to receive "in Christ" lack no good thing.

The Lord has provided everything we need to overcome every obstacle that we face, every day of our lives. The church of the Holy Spirit has more power than anything understood by natural man. We, the church, have significant contributions yet to be made on this earth.

The Japanese could not break the Navajo code, and so too the devil cannot break the code of the Spirit. Speaking in the individual and personal prayer language of the Spirit in what is referred to as "tongues" is a code of heavenly communication that connects us in a vital way with Creator God.

This beautiful language puts us in tune with His heart and mind. Just as only the Navajo Code Talkers could understand each other in their unique, coded tongue, so also does the church as it transmit and receive by the language of the Spirit. As a consequence of this, God also communicates the understanding of those things He would have us to know.[4]

This communication works two ways. It is not God's Spirit speaking to our mind, but rather, God's Spirit to our spirit and our spirit to God's Spirit. We have been given a secure form of communication with the Lord that is one of "the secret counsels which govern God in dealing with the righteous, which are hidden from ungodly and wicked men but plain to the godly."[5]

Through this communication, God speaks His specific plans, purposes, wisdom, instructions, and directions into the life of the Spirit-filled believer. The language of the Holy Spirit is free from danger or harm. It's safe, not liable to fail!

This is a special language, or "code," that cannot be interpreted, understood, or subverted by the enemy. The plan of

---

[4] 1 Corinthians 2:10
[5] *Strong's Concordance*, Strong's Number 3466

the Holy Spirit cannot fail when followed in faith and obedience by the hearer! However, the enemy will nevertheless try to cut off that plan and purpose from our lives and keep it from ever being fulfilled. He acts on knowledge of natural things and spiritual principles. He will try to stop or delay divine help sent for the completion of an appointed task, destination, or provision that is on its way to the believer. Praying in the Spirit is the language of the realm of heaven.

The problem is that people have spiritualized and religionized this gift to such a point of controversy that many have lost sight of its true nature and purpose. It is in this spiritual gift of communication that the dynamite power of God is manifested in and through believers for things that they would not be able to accomplish otherwise. It is through this spiritual language that divine POWER is transmitted!

Chapter 1

THE POWER WITHIN

*"But when the Helper comes, whom I shall send to you
from the Father, the Spirit of truth who proceeds from
the Father, He will testify of Me. And you also will
bear witness, because you have been with Me from the
beginning."*

—*John 15:26–27*

Back in 1948, after completing military service to his country
as a Navajo Code Talker in the Marines, my father was
employed at the base in the small, high desert town of Barstow,
California. It was here that I was born and here that I have
lived my entire life.

As a child, many questions about life stirred within me.
They led me to seek out answers for those curiosities. I believed
God was always with me and I would ask Him many things.
As I grew older, I came to realize that there was a genuine
purpose for my life.

Early on, my father would often take our family to the place
of our natural heritage at Canyon De Chelly on the Navajo
reservation in Arizona. We would stay with my *shi-análí,* or

grandparents, on their land at Del Muerto Canyon. It was there I learned, through the oral tradition handed down from generation to generation, that Native beliefs were based and dependent upon the knowledge of the Great Spirit.

My father was always a man of strong belief in the culture and traditions of the Navajo people. My mother became a born-again believer as a child. She was raised believing the only way to live was to know and follow the Lord Jesus Christ. Faith and the prayers of my mother caused me to come to a place of understanding of the truth and importance of the Word of God in my life. The same Spirit of Truth within her, the Holy Spirit, has revealed to me a greater depth of understanding of the Lord.

The Word of God says, in Jeremiah 29:11,

> *"For I know the thoughts that I think toward you, says the LORD, thoughts of peace and not of evil, to give you a future and a hope."*

In the summer of 1959, my sister and I walked a path down into Canyon Del Muerto with our *grandparents, Shi- náli* to pick corn, melons, apricots, and peaches. We began to journey in a way we had not walked before. In my eyes as a six-year-old child, it seemed as if it would take days to complete the walk.

The pathway was very narrow. It was only about three feet wide. Over the edge of the red-sandstone path was a sheer drop of about seven hundred feet to the canyon floor. My sister and I were terrified and we cried as we walked. My grandmother, *Shi-náli-Asdzáán*, raised her voice at us as we were crying and spoke in Navajo, saying, "Look straight ahead. Do not look down, do not look to the right or to the left," or "Do not look back; look straight ahead!" She repeatedly shouted out to us, "Look straight ahead, one step at a time!"

The Spirit of God speaks these same words to the church today.[6] As we walk this journey of faith with Christ, we are to take one step at a time and not look back.

As the years have gone by, my walk on the path of this spiritual life has been one of always experiencing the goodness of God's love in favor, protection, and faithfulness. Many times, the Holy Spirit has reminded me of those precious words of wisdom *Shi-nálí-Asdzáán* spoke: "Look straight ahead, one step at a time!"

Our heavenly Father has given us One exactly like Jesus. The Holy Spirit of Truth living in us is the Spirit of Christ. He comforts and counsels with the divine instruction of wisdom, for He is the voice of God speaking to believers. Holy Spirit is that One who guides and assists us in our journey down the narrow pathway of life. He causes us to see eye to eye with God! Holy Spirit is our intercessor, our advocate, the one who pleads our case. He is our strengthener. He strengthens us in faith as we pray in the code that cannot be broken. He is our standby. He is to stay with us forever! It is by the Holy Spirit residing in and working through us that God's plans and purposes for our lives are fulfilled.[7]

Well into my young adult years, there were still many questions about life for which I had no answers. Then, in April of 1982, my life was forever transformed when I became a born-again believer in Christ. Jesus became my life partner in this journey down the spiritual path set before me. As I walked with Jesus, I began to receive answers to so many of life's long sought-after questions.

In John 14, we read how Jesus prepares the disciples for His leaving them to go to the Father. He shares great truths about their relationship with Him, the Father, and the Holy Spirit. In

---

[6] Romans 1:17
[7] John 16:13

doing so, He answers many of the disciple's questions and the same questions we have today.

Jesus tells them about Himself by saying, *"I am the way, the truth, and the life. No one comes to the Father except through Me."* Jesus reveals the Father. He includes the truth that the works He does, believers will do also, and they shall be even greater.[8]

As a believer, when that "God-kind of faith" is in you, you can ask anything in His name and He will do it.

My dad has told me that, as a Navajo Code Talker in the war so many years ago, he had to rely on the Great Spirit for the wisdom and guidance he needed to accomplish his mission. Without confident belief in and reliance on the Creator, it would not have been possible. My father has always believed there is a Greater One Who lives within; that One helps and lives in us forever.

Jesus said this very thing.

> *"And I will pray the Father, and He will give you another Helper, that He may abide with you forever."*
> —*John 14:16*

This Helper is the Spirit of our Creator. He is called to one's side. He leads believers to a greater apprehension of gospel truths. In addition to general help and guidance, He gives the strength to endure the hostility of the fallen system of this world.

> *"But when the Helper comes, whom I shall send to you from the Father, the Spirit of truth who proceeds from the Father, He will testify of Me.*
> —*John 15:26*

---

[8] John 14:12

4

*"But the Helper, the Holy Spirit whom the Father will
send in My name, He will teach you all things and bring
to your remembrance all things that I said to you."*
                                                    —*John 14:26*

Jesus told us Holy Spirit will indwell the believer when He
said, *"...the Spirit of truth, whom the world cannot receive, because it
neither sees Him nor knows Him; but you know Him, for He dwells
with you and will be in you,." John 14:17.* The Spirit of Truth is in
you and in me! He will teach you all things and bring to your
remembrance all things that He said to you.

I believe the Spirit of God has brought to my remembrance
that day my *Shi-nálí-Asdzáán* said, "Look straight ahead. Do not
look down, do not look to the right or to the left," and "Do not
look back; look straight ahead!" The Spirit of the Creator will
lead you into greater truths and depths of His Word for the
purpose of bringing you to success in every action in life.

God's Word assures us that

*"...the anointing which you have received from Him
abides in you, and you do not need that anyone teach
you; but as the same anointing teaches you concerning all
things, and is true, and is not a lie, and just as it has
taught you, you will abide in Him."*
                                                    —*1 John 2:27*

The anointing you have received from Him lives in you.
The Holy Spirit is the power of God within you! He provides
the strength needed to endure. He's everything you need. He is
Holy. He represents the very essence of God's nature, personality,
character, and power! Habitually yielding to the influence of
the Holy Spirit causes us to walk in holiness. We can't make

it on our own strength. It was never intended by God that we should. We need Him! Each of us is to be established and built up spiritually. It is the Holy Spirit alone who can accomplish this work as we pray in the code and receive God's Word.

He is who He says He is! By Him are many great and wonderful truths revealed.

When the church comes to perceive and understand the depths of God's plan and align with it, we will see His glory manifested individually and corporately on a scale never seen before!

The Word of God is very powerful. When God's people speak by the Spirit, they have tremendous authority. Authority is defined as the power to settle or determine, the right to control or command.

God's words are like bullets. They have divine power and authority. When His Words are spoken in faith, they penetrate the heavens and God responds.

Although my *shi-análí* didn't know the Bible as we know it, they believed in the Great Creator of all things. They believed that someone created everything in this life. It wasn't man, neither was it a biological accident. It was the Great Spirit.

The Navajo people teach that the world around them is alive and should be treated with respect. It is their goal to keep their world in *"hozho"*, or perfect order.

> *All things were made through Him, and without Him nothing was made that was made.*
> — *John 1:3*

A person's good deeds help maintain that order. On the other hand, thoughtless or cruel actions are believed to destroy nature's order.[9]

---

[9] 1 Timothy. 2:1–2

It is the spoken Word of God in faith that has the ability to move the supernatural power of heaven on one's behalf.

The Bible speaks of three heavens. The first heaven is the natural heaven which is earth. The second heaven is the realm that is felt by the inner spirit of man; not in the natural. The third heaven is, of course, the place of God's throne, where those who die in faith go. When you begin to speak by the Power of His Spirit, the natural earth gives ear; then the second heaven begins to be moved by those words.

As a Native American and by the Word of God, I know this truth is literally life in us. One might ask, "What are you trying to say?" I'm saying what 1 John 2:24 tells us:

> *"Therefore, let that abide in you which you heard from the beginning. If what you heard from the beginning abides in you, you also will abide in the Son and in the Father."*

Native Americans are a particularly spiritual people. There is an inborn understanding within them that there is a Great One; the Great I Am! They understand that they are inwardly connected to their language, the land, and the entire earth. Their language is an inheritance from the Creator, just as much as the land is.

The Navajo people call themselves *Dine'*, which means "the people."

In the Four Corners area of the United States, where Arizona, New Mexico, Utah, and Colorado come together, lies the Navajo reservation. The Navajo have always called this place *Dine'tah*, or land of the people.

In 1864 the US Army forced thousands of Navajos to surrender their homeland. They were made to march 300 miles to Bosque Redondo in New Mexico. The forced march became known as the Long Walk. Many Navajos who were not strong enough to make the journey died along the way.

Back in October 1995, the Spirit of the Lord spoke to me concerning the Long Walk as I was preparing a message to minister at church. He said that during the time of the Long Walk, many cried out to the Great Spirit, the Great I Am. When there is a crying out from our hearts, the Word of God says He hears us.[10] Interestingly enough, when the Navajo people were released from Bosque Redondo, they were allowed to return to the very homeland from which they had been removed. As best as I have been able to find out, this did not happen to any other tribe that went through a similar displacement.

I believe this was a revealing time for those who cried out. The Spirit of God poured out upon the Navajo people. The favor of God was upon them and a great spiritual awakening took place. There may even have been a revival.

The legacy of those events extends directly into my own family. My grandmother was a strong believer in the Great Spirit. She said that although you can't see God, He's there; He's everywhere! These words of hers struck my heart and revealed to me that there is a Creator.

The Amplified Bible translation of John 14:17 reads, *"The Spirit of Truth, Whom the world cannot receive (welcome, take to its heart), because it does not see Him or know and recognize Him. But you know and recognize Him, for He lives with you [constantly] and will be in you."*

In the walk of life's journey, it's clear that many in the Body of Christ fail to discern God's presence or know Him for themselves. For years, the church has relied on pastors and

---

[10] 2 Chronicles 7:14

leaders to hear from God for them. The days of looking entirely to spiritual leaders as if they were Moses is over.

The Lord is raising up mature sons and daughters of the Most High. There is an equipping of the saints to have ears to hear for themselves what the Great Spirit is saying.

The Lord declares to every believer, *"He who has an ear, let him hear what the Spirit says to the churches,"* Revelation 2:7a

The days of ministers holding back an uncompromising Word are over.

Events are coming that the corporate church, needs to prepare for.

The Creator's Spirit, our partner, is constantly urging and nudging us in order to stir and even to shake us to a state of readiness for what is ahead.

It is living our lives "In Christ," that will cause us to endure and to complete our assigned journey.

During the war in the Pacific, my dad was attached to the 5th Marine Division as a Navajo Code Talker. As a good soldier, he reported to his assigned unit for duty, not at Canyon De Chelly, but wherever his commander directed him. He was under assignment with specific instructions.

Many in the church have been given divine assignments but have missed God's path by moving in the wrong direction. It is through obedience to the instructions of God's assignment that He blesses. Obedience and faith, working together, are the keys to the blessings of God.

In Genesis 12:1–3 we read how Abram was instructed to walk in the blessing.

> *"Now the LORD had said to Abram: "Get out of your country,*

From your family, And from your father's house, To a land that I will show you. I will make you a great nation; I will bless you, And make your name great; And you shall be a blessing. I will bless those who bless you, And I will curse him who curses you; And in you all the families of the earth shall be blessed."

It was in this promise that *shi-bizhé'é*, my father, obeyed. He received the blessing. As a young Navajo man he went to war for our nation and was utilized for his language to overcome the enemy. He received the blessing of God for the reward of his obedience. It made a way for him to come out of the despair of poverty he had grown up in and propelled him into a better life for himself and our family.

Similar to Abram, my father left the Navajo land, his family, his father's house to go to another land which God showed him. And so it is for the Body of Christ that when the instructions of kingdom assignment are followed, the blessings follow.

It is time, church, that we fulfill our calling and true purpose! It's time to be a pipeline through which the glory of God can flow and be the testimony of the greatness of His love, faithfulness, and power. The Power of the Spirit within you can give you the ability to fulfill that calling.

After the Japanese surprise attack on American forces stationed at Pearl Harbor in 1941, the Commander of the Japanese fleet, Admiral Yamamoto, was said to have stated, "I fear all we have done is to awaken a sleeping giant and fill him with a terrible resolve."

There was a time, it is written, when there were giants in the land. They were seen as a formidable enemy in the natural.[11]

---

[11] Numbers 13:33

Joel 3:9 says,

"Proclaim this among the nations: "Prepare for war!
Wake up the mighty men, Let all the men of war draw
near, Let them come up."

The body of Christ has been sleeping in complacency for
far too long. Are you mighty men in these last days? I believe
the day has come in which the church should arise and say, "We
are giants in the Spirit. We shall rise up as giants." Awaken
sleeping giant; awaken mighty men!

Over the course of many years, I have been given dozens
of prophetic dreams which the Lord has used to guide and
assist me in dealing with important issues. In March of 1995,
I had such a dream that relates to this area of concern. In my
dream there were two beautiful white church buildings. Each
was identical to the other. Half of the people of the church
were in one building and the other half in the second building.
The church was divided. A house divided against itself cannot
stand.[12]

I walked into the building to the right and the people
were lying in beds and on mattresses on the floor. It was as
though they had no desire to seek God. I looked around and
recognized many people in the church whom I knew. They
were comfortable and resting.

Then I walked out of that building and into the building on
the left. The doors were locked. I knocked on the window to the
right of the door to get the attention of the people inside. They
saw me knocking at the window but stood motionless and would
not unlock the door. I heard this: "My Spirit is not welcome in

---

[12] Mark 3:25

the church." When the Spirit of God is in the church, change is required.

The church at large does not want change. It wants to hold on to the doctrines and traditions of men while rejecting the true wisdom of God. In doing so it denies the forward leading of the Spirit of God. It is in the demonstration of His power that the Holy Spirit is manifested.

The body of Christ has been sleeping for years. Now is the time! "Awake Oh sleeper!"

Chapter 2

SPIRITUAL AWAKENING

"And do this, knowing the time, that now it is high time to awake out of sleep; for now our salvation is nearer than when we first believed."

—*Romans 13:11*

As the thundering sounds of war were heard among the young Navajo Code Talkers, thoughts of their own mortality drew them closer to the Creator than they ever imagined they would be. Inwardly, there was a genuine awakening.

It is high time for the church in America to awaken out of the deep sleep it has been in for far too long! The church is to be sober-minded, alert, and watchful of the plans and movements of the enemy in these last days.

"Therefore let us not sleep, as others do, but let us watch and be sober."

—*1 Thessalonians 5:6*

As the Code Talkers went about accomplishing their assignments, they were thoroughly aware of the enemy and the dangers that were ever present.

Much of the church today is not even aware of the genuine dangers they face or the enemy's tactics. Tragically, Christians are generally not taught about the depth and wealth of the finished redemptive work of Christ which was made available to them when they were saved. They are not made aware of their true, God-given identity "in Christ." They are not instructed in how to exercise the delegated authority of Christ to enforce the victory He has already obtained for them. Therefore, they never really develop their inner man to become spiritually mature.

> *"For everyone who partakes only of milk is unskilled in the word of righteousness, for he is a babe. But solid food belongs to those who are of full age, that is, those who by reason of use have their senses exercised to discern both good and evil."*
>
> *—Hebrews 5:13–14*

Many times, leaders turn the other way to avoid confrontation and critically needed change because of blind adherence to doctrines of men that make the Word of God powerless. Still others are more interested in a self-serving position that they believe will be of minimal cost. But in the end, their place is one of darkness and weeping and gnashing of teeth.[13]

The enemy continually comes to hinder or even abort the plan of God, while the church stands by trying to figure out what went wrong.

---

[13] Matthew 8:12

"However, when He, the Spirit of truth, has come, He will guide you into all truth; for He will not speak on His own authority, but whatever He hears He will speak; and He will tell you things to come."

—*John 16:13*

Many in the family of God have ignorantly or even knowingly allowed the enemy to derail or destroy their walk to fulfilling their God-given purpose in life. Remember, Christ in you is greater than the devil who lives in the world.[14] Jesus said, "My house shall be called a house of prayer." You are that house, Christian![15] However, this can be true only when the people of God come under His authority and align themselves in agreement with God's Word, which is His will. God is calling the church to its rightful and most important place, the place of prayer!

Part of the church is crying out for the "end time, latter rain" of God and His Kingdom to come. The other part has forgotten about the critical role of repentance and is relying on grace to cover them, even in a lifestyle of habitual sin. Thank God for His Grace. But His grace, in this context, covers us when we miss the mark and gets us back on track; it does not promote a state of continual disobedience.

In 2 Chronicles 7:14, His Word to the church is clear and simple.

"If My people who are called by My name will humble themselves, and pray and seek My face, and turn from their wicked ways, then I will hear from heaven, and will forgive their sin and heal their land."

---

[14] 1 John 4:4
[15] Matthew 21:13

It has been preached to the body of Christ for years that Christians have become deaf and numb to the instructions and directions given by the Spirit of God. The destructive spirit of pride has become so entrenched in the church that it has caused the people of God to be deceived to the point that they are incapable of discerning His presence and yielding to His direction for the Body of Christ.

The Psalmist asks the question, *"Who may ascend into the hill of the LORD? Or who may stand in His holy place?"* The answer comes in verse four. *"He who has clean hands and a pure heart, who has not lifted up his soul to an idol, Nor sworn deceitfully." Psalm 24:3–4*

The Spirit of our Creator has given us such wonderful insight into His beautiful Word.

The church has become absorbed with comfort and self-satisfaction which leads to idolatry. Anything in our lives to which we give preference over following the heart of God is an idol. Many people have become their own idols in the worship of self-interest. They are mostly unaware of their existing moral deficiencies and the spiritual dangers that prevent them from becoming the awesome powerhouse for God that they are meant to be in our nation. Many of our spiritual and governmental leaders have sworn deceitfully by accepting as true what God has clearly called sin.

America is a nation that was founded on the covenant Word of God. And so, we, as Americans living in a blessed nation, are called upon to be a praying nation, a God-fearing nation! Without repentance and the surrendering of oneself to God, there can be no meaningful change.

Godly change for the individual and the nation comes from praying people who are awake and receptive to the leading of the Spirit. They are alerted to the pitfalls intended for their destruction!

We, the people of God, are called to be on the front lines, to be that house of prayer. It is sad to say that many become terribly distracted by focusing on their own wounds, offenses, and issues. This has caused Christians to stop praying and as a result have laid down their spiritual weapon of warfare.

The Code Talkers were on the front lines. Although these Navajo Marines had experienced loss of land and relatives in the Long Walk, they remembered and kept the oath of allegiance to the United States. They understood that they had made a covenant vow when they enlisted in the military to fight for their nation. Yet they still gave their allegiance and committed to be vessels for our nation, becoming yielded instruments used to win the war.

They had volunteered to fight and even die for a nation that had historically wounded and robbed them and treated them with contempt.

This is the enemy's tactic! He will take what is not his, by taking what rightfully belongs to you in order to strip you and prevent you from fulfilling your assigned destiny.

The church often experiences lack and loss as it goes through trials. Many become discouraged, lay down their spiritual weapons, and simply give up. Making the critical decision not to quit, no matter what, and to hold fast to God's truth throughout life's trials will build character and faith. This is necessary to equip us to fight the good fight of faith.[16] It causes us to become the overcomers we were created to be in Christ.

The Code Talkers experienced trials in their mission and learned that without the Great Creator, they would not be able to endure and overcome the enemy.

---

[16] 1 Timothy 6:12

17

Somehow, the people of God tend to forget the covenant they entered into when they invited the Spirit of Christ to come and live in their hearts. This is a covenantal vow much like the marriage vow, "Till death do us part."

Navajo Code Talkers were given instruction and direction in regards to using their language gift to help win the war. The language was the code. The code was the gift. A code is a simple, systematic collection of rules and procedures or conduct. When these systematic rules and procedures are properly used, they bring about a desired result. In order for the Navajo Code Talkers to accomplish their mission, they had to obey the commands given them.

The church is on a mission. That mission is a Kingdom assignment. There are commands in the Word of God, to be interpreted by the Holy Spirit, which we are to follow in order to complete this assignment. The Lord spoke to the prophet Jeremiah, saying, *"Obey My voice, and do according to all that I command you; so shall you be My people, and I will be your God."* — *Jeremiah 7:23*

When we obey God, He makes sure we are taken care of. There is protection! There is a formula. It is a God-given, spiritual process that works to bring restoration to the people and to the land. But it only works if the people are willing and obedient.[17] Only then will we see divine results.

To aid this restoration, a code has been given to every believer, just as there was a code for the Navajo Code Talkers. This code cannot be broken because the enemy cannot break it. The formula is found in 2 Chronicles 7:14. It is intended to be the accepted means, without objection, for accomplishing restoration.

---

[17] Isaiah 1:19

Over 2,400 years ago, God told His people that if they would: humble themselves and pray, seek His face and turn from their wicked ways (repent and go in the opposite direction); then He would hear their prayers and forgive their sins and heal their land.

This is a formula summarized by five basic characteristics: humility, obedience, prayer, purity, and expectation.

Humility is God's style. What is humility? It is defined as honesty, lowliness, a sense of moral insignificance, and unselfish concern for the welfare of others. It is a total absence of arrogance, conceit, or haughtiness.

Only by being renewed in their minds, abstaining from self-exaltation, and from being puffed up in pride can members of the Christian community obtain and maintain unity and harmony.[18]

The Navajo Code Talkers did not join the military to lift themselves up and say, "Look what we did!" These young men went in humbly, but with confidence, and they trusted in the Creator. They volunteered to fight for their homeland, not knowing they would become Code Talkers.

Haughtiness has come into the church today like a flood. The Word of God says, *"When the enemy comes in like a flood, the Spirit of God will lift up a standard against Him."* —*Isaiah 59:19*

It is that sense of pride in superiority that makes haughtiness infectious like a disease. It brings defeat to the people of God. God resists the proud only because the proud resist God. When we exalt the Word in ourselves as we walk in that Word and die to self in the process, and we allow the Word to release its power in us, it is then lifted above all else.

Pride and haughtiness are a distraction, a tool the enemy uses to hold Christians back in their efforts to complete their

---

[18] Romans 12:1–2

kingdom assignment. In our nation today, many are allowing the enemy to rob them of the ability to move toward the high calling in Christ and to walk worthy of that calling to which they were called with all lowliness and gentleness, with longsuffering, and bearing with one another in love, endeavoring to keep the unity of the Spirit in the bond of peace.[19]

Christ intended that there should be unity in His body with singleness of heart, mind, and will. The Word clearly says, *"There is one body and one Spirit, just as you were called in one hope of your calling; one Lord, one faith, one baptism; one God and Father of all, who is above all, and through all, and in you all. —Ephesians 4:4–6*

Spiritual unity was key to the life and teachings of the early church, and so it is today. Our goal is to do everything possible to keep and preserve the unity of the Spirit. We are to *"all speak the same thing, and that there be no divisions among us, but that we be perfectly joined together in the same mind and in the same judgment."*[20] As one true church, we are admonished to lift up the standard! Keep the unity of the Spirit and pray so that we see results.

We are living in the end of the present age, when we have been forewarned of end-time events. There is a real awakening taking place in our nation. God has a plan and it is taking place exactly as He has designed. The apostle Paul speaks of the responsibility of the church when he says that when the church prays in faith, God will respond and move. He writes, *"Therefore I exhort first of all that supplications, prayers, intercessions, and giving of thanks be made for all men, for kings and all who are in authority, that we may lead a quiet and peaceable life in all godliness and reverence. For this is good and acceptable in the sight of God our Savior."* [21] We are to pray for all men, for Kings, and for those in authority—not just

---

[19] Ephesians 4:1–3

[20] 1 Corinthians 1:10

[21] 1 Timothy 2:1–3

once, but continuously. When you pray, there are good results. If there is no prayer of faith in God, wickedness prevails!

The Native American Code Talkers believed in prayer. Native Americans are true believers in prayer. There is no doubt that the Code Talkers prayed. My dad and my uncle, who were both Navajo Code Talkers, both told me about how they prayed. They relied on God to protect them and on the Creator to show them a plan of good results. Although accounts vary, it has been stated that only as few as 13 out of about 420 Code Talkers died in WWII.

The decline of America's spiritual health is not only marked by the outlawing of Christian prayer in our public schools, but by the absence of concerted, fervent prayer in the church. Just call a prayer meeting and see what percentage of the people show up. The church has largely become an entertainment center.

Back in September of 2009, we invited a man of God to come to our church and minister. As people came in and filled up the seats, the Spirit of the Lord spoke to me. His question was this: "Would you rather have this or My power?" This was a wake-up call for me because the priority of so many pastors and ministers—myself included—is to pack the church full of people. But a large number of people in a church doesn't necessarily mean that the power of God will be manifested. My realization was that a church can be full of people, yet powerless.

For the most part, the power of God is absent in the church today. Without His power the church is only a group, a club, or an organization that meets every week and, if allowed, twice a week. Many people come to church to hear a certain person or to be entertained. The church needs prayer in the house. Those in authority need prayer. Everything starts with the leadership and flows all the way down to the body.

The Code Talkers did not fulfill their assignment for the purposes of entertainment. Those young Marines never thought they would be known or recognized for their commitment and service. In their minds, they were just doing their jobs.

Our prayers make a difference. These are the last days before the return of the Lord, and God wants to bring all who would come into His Kingdom. This includes those in authority, from the greatest to the least, from the president of our nation all the way down to the neediest of all. Christ has redeemed His people *"out of every tribe and tongue and people and nation."*[22]

The church in general needs a revelation of what God's Kingdom is. There is currently a spiritual awakening, a shaking, in which the Kingdom of God is being revealed. The intent is for there to be a transformation in the body of Christ, a change of heart, a new heart, a heart of flesh, not of stone. No one has all the answers except God. It all starts with prayer. More than ever, we're seeing purely academic and intellectual examination of the Bible's truths.

The result is a system of philosophical doctrines of men which lack the contribution of the Holy Spirit that comes by trust in God and intimate relationship with Him.

The Code Talkers completed their assignment. Each and every one of us is called by God to complete His Kingdom assignment. Our prayers are what make a difference in our lives. James 5:16 reads, *"The effective, fervent prayer of a righteous man avails much."* The people who make up the true church are the righteous. The church's prayers avail much. The definition of "to avail" is to be of use, advantage, or value to; to be of effective use in the achievement of a goal. The church has value.

---

[22] Revelation 5:9

The Code Talkers had great value. Their language was a gift. The Navajo language code had value and profited our whole nation. It was used greatly as an effective tool to achieve the goal of ultimate victory over the enemy of the American people. There was power in the language, not just as a code, but because Creator God gave this language by the Holy Spirit. We know this because John 1:3 tells us, *"All things were made through Him, and without Him, nothing was made that was made."*

Our dependence is to be upon Creator God for all things.

The Church is called to a place of prayer. It is a place of being dependent upon God and on Him alone. When the value of effective, fervent prayer becomes a reality in the church, then also will the ministry begin to understand the value and critical nature of the ministry of reconciliation.

It is the reconciliation of all the disjointed and separated members of the church that will bring about the true agreement and harmony required for the corporate power of God to be unleashed against the plans and schemes of the enemy.

When the Code Talkers were in the midst of the war, there was harmony among them. Without harmony, there is chaos. Orders were given in a consistent, orderly manner by those in authority and then were received and carried out by the Code Talkers.

God is our authority and He has a consistent, orderly manner by which He delivers orders to His church, even as those orders are received and carried out by obedient saints.

The Code Talkers have a testimony of the faithfulness of their Creator because they overcame the enemy and they did not love their lives, even to the death. They willingly laid down their lives in sacrifice for our nation.

> *"And they overcame him by the blood of the Lamb and by the word of their testimony, and they did not love their lives to the death."*
>
> —Revelation *12:11*

Unfortunately, more than ever, we see Christians idolize their own wants and desires above God's. The people of the church tend to look only to pastors and leaders for spiritual guidance rather than first seeking the counsel of the Holy Spirit and the fruits of studying the Word of God. Leaders have answers, but our Lord and Savior's answers for us are much greater!

The children of Israel looked upon Moses as their God. They idolized Him. They expected Moses to hear from God for them. Their seeking was limited to, "Moses, what did God say?" This sounds a lot like the church today! The church is looking to leaders to hear from God for them.

In all this something wonderful is happening. Believers are being supernaturally awakened. God is awakening them to their condition of spiritual weakness and inability that has overtaken them. Disobedience in relationship with the Lord Jesus has been at the root.

People are experiencing an inward urging to rededicate and consecrate their lives to Christ; they are returning to the place of right standing with God. This shaking is awakening the people of God from the apathy and spiritual slumber that they have allowed to set in.

No prayer, no results! Much prayer, much results!

Divine change and a shifting is on the way. God tells us that He will *"Yet once more ... remove those things that are being shaken, as of things that are made, that the things which cannot be shaken may remain.*[23] In His great mercy and love, God is shaking the earth and even heaven in order to remove anything and everything that would hinder His kingdom from being perfectly complete.

It seems that for the most part, the church has forgotten the covenant it made with God to be completely yielded to Him, body, soul, and spirit. When this covenant is broken, it opens the door to judgment. Sin provokes judgment. Judgment comes against the sin. Why? Because sin separates God from relationship with man, the object of His love.

Who is responsible for a nation in decline or a city going down? As the church family goes, so goes the nation. Righteousness will bring praise to a nation or a people. But sin brings disapproval and shame.[24]

Why is this? It's because change comes through prayer. The church has become slack in prayer. The prayers of God's covenant people are what cause change for the better. We are on an assignment called a "Kingdom assignment." This assignment can only be successfully completed through close, intimate contact with the Lord in prayer. It's in the direct communication of prayer that God reveals His plans and provides strategies for the assignment. Through prayer, God responds to those who belong to Him and forewarns of what is ahead.

Thank God for His longsuffering and mercy. There is a remnant of the church that is crying out for mercy for all. God truly is merciful. *"His mercy is new every morning"* (Lamentations 3:23). He delights in mercy. God looks for a man, one man to stand in the gap on behalf of the people of the land.

In Ezekiel 22:30–31, God reveals how He *"...sought for a man among them who would make a wall, and stand in the gap before*

---

[23] Hebrews 12:27

[24] Proverbs 14:34

*Me on behalf of the land, that I should not destroy it; but I found no one.
Therefore I have poured out My indignation on them; I have consumed
them with the fire of My wrath; and I have recompensed their deeds on
their own heads, says the Lord GOD."*

We see here that the laws and statutes of God are broken.
Judgment starts in the house of God, not in our nation. When
God sees judgment coming upon a nation, the first thing He
does is search for a man—not a multitude, but one man!

It is difficult to get a multitude of people to agree even on
what time of day it is. The issue is not the quantity of people
but the quality of the character of the people. There is one body
of people in Christ. That one body, commissioned by God, is
capable of changing the course of a nation. Moses did!

A nation is a body of people associated with a territory.
How great would it be for a people to come back to the place of
prayer in the demonstration of the power of God? The church
can change the nation. God always desires to show mercy!

Church, God is stirring His people so that the Body of
Christ and America should awake! The devil greatly fears the
omnipotent power potential of the praying church. He fears
that God will awaken the sleeping giant of the church and fill
it with a terrible resolve.

The church has a place of standing in Jesus Christ. The
church has gained this position by making Jesus their Savior
and Lord. But where greater position is gained, responsibility
is also added.

In the book of Genesis, we read the account of Abraham
interceding for Sodom.[25]

God is so loving and desires not to have to judge sin. If
He had wanted to execute judgment on Sodom, why did He

---

[25] Genesis18:16–33

tell Abraham what He was doing? Because He knew what Abraham would do! Abraham stood in the gap. This is love! Love covers a multitude of sins. God's heart's desire was to see judgment averted and the city saved.

Our nation is living in a time of compromise and justification of sinful decisions and actions. Sin and wickedness are running rampant everywhere we look. I believe God is shaking up the church so there will be a crying out of repentance for mercy! The cry for mercy, in faith, pushes back judgment.

We, as the church, have a great position of responsibility, a place assigned to us. That place is the place of prayer.

As the young Code Talkers cried out to God from their assigned place in the war, He heard their cries. As those cries went forth, the Code Talkers reminded God of their forefathers, who had prayed to the Great Spirit to protect their sons and daughters from any kind of harm.

"I have set watchmen on your walls, O Jerusalem; They shall never hold their peace day or night. You who make mention of the LORD, do not keep silent, And give Him no rest till He establishes And till He makes Jerusalem a praise in the earth."

—*Isaiah 62:6–7*

These warriors spoke out the promise God made with them and did not remain silent! As they spoke and released the power of their faith, it in turn gave them the strength and ability to move forward in the covenant they had made with our God, for our nation. That promise was precious and held much authority and power.

Chapter 3

THE GIFT

"He who speaks from himself seeks his own glory; but He who seeks the glory of the One who sent Him is true, and no unrighteousness is in Him."

—*John 7:18*

It was back in 2006 that I had a dream of a gift in glossy red paper with a gold ribbon tied into a big, beautiful bow on top. The gift was floating in place about two feet off the floor in front of me and to my right as I stood on the platform.

Directly to my right was a row of five microphones on stands without anyone behind them. To the left of me was a keyboard, also without anyone behind it. I was in a place that looked very much like an old theatre with stadium-style seating. Some people were randomly scattered about in the seats while others were standing in the aisles. They were all mingling with one another in their little groups.

Although no words were being spoken I was fully aware of what was taking place. I was able to recognize people and understand their actions.

There were three people standing in the aisle behind the seats at the top right hand corner of the building. They were looking out the windows, giving their full attention to what was going on outside.

These three were praise and worship team members.

The ground started to shake as in an earthquake. I noticed the people were not focused on the purpose of the gathering. Everyone was more focused on each other. As the ground shook, the gift shook as well, even though it was still hovering above the ground. Within myself, I heard, "Pray! Pray in your spiritual language, with authority!" As I prayed, I went to one of the microphones and spoke, but it was as if no one could hear me. I went to the next microphone and again, no one was able to hear me. I went to the third and fourth microphones with the same results.

Then I went to the fifth and last microphone, and I raised my voice. It was as if the Holy Spirit in me raised His voice. Then the people were able to hear. Spiritual ears were unplugged. I looked at the lady in the front row, to the left of me, and I yelled, "Get in your place! Get in your position behind the keyboard!"

When we humbly get into God's appointed position for our lives, we remove the restrictions that we place upon Him through the exercise of self-will that's not in agreement with His will. In turn, our hindrances are then taken out of the way. Then the Holy Spirit is able to clearly communicate His will to us without interference.

(There is more to the dream. However, I can only share as much of the interpretation as I am led to share at this time.)

This is what I heard the Spirit of God speak: "There is a shaking going on individually and corporately in the house of God." The gifts in the church are being shaken. There has also been a spirit of deafness upon God's people, preventing them from receiving instructions. God encourages us to hear when He says, *"He who has an ear, let him hear what the Spirit says to the churches."*[26]

There is a choice the church must make. People need to ask themselves, "Am I going to move on His Word or not?" If they decide not to act in removing hindrances identified to them, they are choosing not to hear or obey the Lord. They then receive spiritual deafness instead. Remember, not until I prayed through the fifth microphone did the people hear. The number five is symbolic for grace. By the grace of God, some are able to hear. It wasn't until I prayed with boldness in the authority of His power that the ground and the gift quit shaking.

Some in the church are not in the proper position for the Holy Spirit to utilize them. There are those who are present in the church but not operating in their divinely appointed position. The result is that they interfere with God's plan for their lives. This interference can even extend to hinder God's Spirit from moving in the corporate body as He would choose.

The church is looking to be entertained. The three people I mentioned who were looking out the window were praise and worship team members. They were more interested in being entertained by what was going on outside than in what God was doing inside. They were so distracted by entertainment and self-interest that there was no focus on the Word or on the prayer taking place.

Did you know that the more you pray, the more shaking occurs? This is because when, at the crossroads of decision, we allow the Holy Spirit to show us the things in our lives that hinder or distract us from effectively moving forward and we respond in obedience, we come further under the Lord's

---

[26] Revelation 2:7a

leadership. The Spirit of God not only reveals the problems in our lives, but also empowers us to make the necessary corrections.

In my dream, the gift was shaking. The gift of ministry, the gift of leadership, the gift of worship, the gift of helps—every gift in the church was being shaken. The church is in the midst of a great shaking.

Speaking of the time that is upon us, God foretells, " ... *Once more (it is a little while) I will shake heaven and earth, the sea and dry land; and I will shake all nations, and they shall come to the Desire of All Nations, and I will fill this temple with glory,' says the* LORD *of hosts. 'The silver is Mine, and the gold is Mine,' says the* LORD *of hosts. 'The glory of this latter temple shall be greater than the former,' says the* LORD *of hosts. 'And in this place I will give peace,' says the* LORD *of hosts."—Haggai 2:6–9*

Many of us have experienced the glory of the Lord in the past. It was good; it was powerful, it was awesome! But the glory we're about to experience is greater.

In March of 1995, I preached at the church we were attending. The anointing was so strong that after we got home at around 10:30 at night, I couldn't sleep. It was as if I was "high as a Georgia Pine," as my father-in-law used to say. I felt like my feet were not even touching the floor. It was as if I were floating. I paced around in the house all night, praying in my spiritual language until about five in the morning. My flesh could not handle the anointing any longer and I fell to my knees in the kitchen and yelled out, "Lord, take this from me!"

It was as if a wind blew right through me, from the bottom of my feet to the top of my head. It actually had a sound to it. I said, "Lord, what is this?" This is what I heard: "You've experienced my 'glory' in a measure of a grain of salt and your flesh could not handle it."

The church is crying out for God's glory to come and yet it is living in a place of compromise. Remember the story of Ananias and Saphira? Together, they lied to the apostle Peter about the amount of money they received for the sale of some of their property. What they didn't realize was that the glory of God was so manifest in that place that they were actually lying directly to the Holy Spirit Himself. Both Ananias and Saphira dropped dead after their lie was exposed by the Holy Spirit through Peter.[27] When the presence of the glory of God is manifest in the church, it exposes all the things that should have been shaken off, but weren't. So, as the church cries out for His glory to come, we are asking for every bit of darkness to be exposed. When the glory comes, the light shines!

We should be careful what we ask for. Thank God for His grace! He is preparing the church for His glory, which we read about in Haggai 2:9: *"'The glory of this latter temple shall be greater than the former,' says the LORD of hosts. 'And in this place I will give peace,' says the LORD of hosts."* Do you want peace? I sure do!

The ways of fleshly thinking and living must decrease so that He may increase in us!

We will live in this glory for eternity. When that day comes, when we leave this place called earth, we will step right into eternity. And so, our fleshly living is to die so we may step right into this spiritual place called heaven.

In Haggai's day, the temple building spoken of was a physical building. Today, that building is you and me, individually and corporately, as the church.

Back in 1944, during the war, the Code Talkers wanted peace. They asked themselves, "Where are we headed? Why

---

[27] Acts 5:1–11

are we doing what we're doing? What are we doing for our nation? Is this the Creator's will?"

These young warriors understood covenant. What is covenant? It is a formal agreement between two or more parties to do or not to do something specified. Scripture identifies the conditional promises of covenant made to all humanity by God. Covenant is a legally binding agreement, especially one under seal or pledge. A covenant is made once we invite the Spirit of Christ to live in us. It is, in essence, like a marriage vow in which two commit completely in love and loyalty to each other.

The Code Talkers committed their loyalty to the cause out of love for our country. There was no turning back for them once they made that pledge and vowed to serve our country; there was no way out but death. Once you're in, you're in. All the wounds and hurt of the past had to be laid down. They had to get rid of prejudice in order to function in a covenant environment. Once a covenant is made, it will protect you from prejudice forever, if it's maintained properly.

This is what the church missed in the Native American Indian. The Native American is a covenant-minded man who saw a great people in the Americans, who had more ideas than he had ever dreamed of, a people who lived in ways far beyond what he had ever known.

Just after we were married in 1979, my husband and I went to the Navajo reservation. There I introduced him to many of my family members who lived on the "rez." One of his first introductions was to my father's parents. My grandpa, *Shi-nálí-Hastíín*, welcomed my husband into the family.

During the course of the visit, my husband asked my grandfather when he was born. As my grandfather did not speak English, he replied in Navajo. He said he didn't know the month or year except that it was six summers after the Long

33

Walk. My husband looked up when the Long Walk took place and discovered that the return of the Navajo to the canyon happened in 1868. That made my grandfather about 105 years old at that time.

Shi-náli-Hastíín (grandfather) showed appreciation and respect to my husband because he believed that white men were smart and capable of accomplishing anything they put their mind to. When they met, *Shi-náli-Hastíín* took his bolo tie off his neck, put it on my husband, and said, *"Yá'át'ééh,"* which means welcome in Navajo. He looked at me and said, in Navajo, "You did a beautiful job." He wanted to know what my husband was like, where he came from, and how he thought. My grandfather made a covenant with my husband that day when he welcomed my husband into the family.

For the most part, the church does not understand the concept of covenant. When a covenant is made, it is for life, "till death do us part." We are equally responsible for our brothers in Christ. There should be no jealousy or competition within the church. Sadly, this is where the church has fallen very short. People remain divided by all the things they can be divided by, and therefore, they will not and cannot come together to be of the same mind.[28] Because of this, the Spirit is grieved and He withdraws. The effect is that there is little to no corporate power present in the body as a whole.

God desires to pour out great glory upon all His children! But it will not happen if the church competes with one another and the gifts of God in the church are used to glorify man rather than God.

The gift was shaking in the church! There are many gifts in the church and the shaking is causing people to release

---

[28] 1 Corinthians 1:10

things out of their lives that are not of Him. Only those things that *are* of the Kingdom shall remain. We are to be *"doers of the Word,"* –James 1:20. This is the purpose for the shaking: that we may do His Word and not be hearers only.

God is shaking the church! How? By His voice! The voice within us is the Holy Spirit of God, and we must listen as we allow His voice to speak.

The young Marine warriors had a voice. The voice within them was a gift, a language that had power and authority, one that the enemy could not understand. The enemy could not break the code of this language.

Nor can the enemy understand this Holy language of heaven within you. The Word of God says: *"My people are destroyed for lack of knowledge."*[29] This gift within us is a great benefit we possess in Christ. The beautiful Holy Spirit of God that lives in us has much power, and the gift of this spiritual language is given to us freely! Through it, He takes us to greater depths of understanding in Him.

Jesus directed us to pray, *"Your Kingdom come, Your will be done on earth as it is in Heaven."*[30] The Kingdom of God is the domain of the Holy Spirit and the Kingdom is within each believer. Each of us should be very sober concerning these things because we are given warning.

In Hebrews 12:25-27 it reads: *"See that you do not refuse Him who speaks. For if they did escape who refused Him who spoke on earth, much more shall we not escape if we turn away from Him who speaks from heaven whose voice then shook the earth; but now He has promised, saying, "Yet once more I shake not only the earth, but also heaven. Now this, yet once more, indicates the removal of those things that are being*

---

[29] Hosea 4:6
[30] Matthew 6:10

shaken as of things that are made, that the things which cannot be shaken may remain.""

—Whose voice shook the earth? God's voice.

This is the Kingdom! Remember that it says, *"Yet once more I shake not only the earth, but also heaven."* There is a Kingdom in Heaven where Christ rules and reigns, and that same Kingdom is in the earth, resident inside those who are in Christ. The Kingdom is on the earth as well as in heaven, and the Kingdom is within you and me!

The Kingdom is simply manifest through the unshakeable Lordship of Jesus Christ, who rules and governs the established hearts of men. The things of God, built upon the foundation of Christ, shall endure all the shaking and remain. Do you see that we're to be imitators of Jesus, who is the living Word of God? We cannot truly imitate Him if there are things in us that are not of Him and if we refuse to surrender and let go of them. It is the influence of the Holy Spirit inside us that causes our spirit man to resemble the Word.

The very definition of the word "imitate" is to follow as a model or example, to mimic (say everything the Holy Spirit says), to impersonate, to copy, to reproduce clearly. We are to imitate the author's style. The author is Jesus.

Is the Holy Spirit in you? If it is, then the Kingdom is alive in you as well. Heaven lives in you and you are well able to be utilized by Him, as an imitator of Him.

The Code Talkers were utilized by our God. Everything these young warriors did in the time of war was a plan of God. They were utilized to help win the war. Every one of them was used by our Creator. No one was greater than another. They worked together as committed warriors with a purpose and a goal. There was unity; there had to be unity for victory.

The people of the church are called together to work as committed warriors with a purpose and a goal to prepare the way for the return of the Lord! When there is unity, there is great power.

The outcome of the war in the Pacific was victory.

God's plan for the church is for us also, to be victors! The war has already been won. The people of the church have to see this by the eye of the Spirit Kingdom which lives in them.

The Code Talkers had to picture themselves as victorious in order to achieve a victorious outcome.

The Creator Spirit is a precious gift to us! A gift is something given voluntarily without payment in return, the act of giving something without its being bought or earned by the receiver. The Holy Spirit has freely given us gifts. These are the word of wisdom, the word of knowledge, the gift of faith, the gift of healings, the working of prophecy, the discerning of spirits, to another different kinds of tongues and the interpretation of tongues.[31] These gifts are all precious.

The gift in my dream was beautiful, glossy, shiny red with a ribbon that was pure gold. Red is symbolic of the blood of Jesus and of passion. These gifts were bought for us with His blood that was shed on the cross in order that we may be passionate for Him. The gold ribbon stands for purity and riches. He shakes off of you those things that do not belong, that are not of Him, so that you may be pure.

Jesus paid for the gift that is in you: the Holy Spirit. He laid down His life for you that you might possess all His gifts. He also sees you as a gift to Himself! Gifts are precious, and He sees you as precious. How would you feel if you got to heaven

---

[31] 1 Corinthians 12:8–10

and found out there were gifts in you, deposited at the new birth, that you had never opened, let alone known were there?

Many in the church have gifts but never use them. Gifts are blessings. The Lord's blessing is our greatest gift and wealth!

Psalm 112:3 tells us: *"Wealth and riches will be in his house, and His righteousness endures forever."*

The gift within you may be a special ability, a talent, a gift of music, a gift to teach, or a gift of helps. These gifts are placed in you by God and are resident. When the shaking comes, those things that are of the Kingdom will remain. Heaven and earth are shaking, just as in my dream, the ground was shaking and the gift was shaking. There was an earthquake in the church. It wasn't until prayer by the unction of the Holy Spirit went forth that the ground and the gift quit shaking.

Remember that in the dream, it was as if I was communicating by the Spirit. I yelled out, "Get in your place!" People have to be in their place appointed to them by God. There is a place for each individual in Christ's body, the church. It's not a game of musical chairs, where someone is always left out. In much the same way, on the human body, there is a specific place for every body part, designed as a perfect fit; there is only one place on my body for my right hand to be.

Some people are not in place. Remember Haggai 2:9: *"And in this place I will give peace,' says the Lord of hosts."* The definition of "place" is a particular portion of space and time. It is a space or seat for a person; a position; a situation; a location. It is that which is set aside for a specific purpose. Haggai is speaking of the temple of God, which you are![32]

You have the greatest degree of grace, peace, blessing, and protection when you are in the place He has called you to.

---

[32] 1 Corinthians 3:16

Remember the microphones in my dream? It was not until I went behind the fifth microphone and prayed with the authority of God's Word that the people were able to hear. It was as if they were deaf.

The fifth microphone has significance. The number five is symbolic of grace. God has given us the grace that has brought us through to the present time. Now we are in an accelerated time! The clock is ticking. We're in a high level of grace right now; however, grace does not give us license to sin. It empowers you to overcome the sin. The church must walk in Him, in His love!

Prayer works. Prayer changes things. It can cause the shaking to stop or it can make it continue. The Creator's Spirit within you knows what is needed. He shakes off the hindrances that don't belong in our lives.

I've preached this message on a couple of different reservations and actually brought a beautiful red box with a gold ribbon, just like the one I dreamed. I took the gift and shook it and asked the church, "What could be in it? Have you ever thought the Lord would take you and shake you? I have. Could there be unforgiveness, jealousy, gossip, selfish ambition inside it? Hmm ... some pride, perhaps?" He may shake you and say, "Oh, no, no, no! This does not belong!" Why would He do this? So that the church, i.e., you and I, may remain clean and pure before Him.

Every gift is being shaken: the gift of ministries, the gift of leadership, the gift of helps. Church, there is a gift in you!

First Peter 4:10 reads, *"As each one has received a gift, minister it to one another, as good stewards of the manifold grace of God. It says each one has received a gift."*

That gift was birthed in you at conception. Before you even went through the birth canal, He knew you. "Good stewards" refers to Christians in general using the gifts the Lord has entrusted them with for the strengthening and encouraging of fellow believers. As brothers and sisters in Christ, we are to encourage and strengthen one another.

We are His workmanship created in Him for good works.[33] God says that you didn't find Him; He found you! He found you in the middle of your sin, whether it was drugs, partying, or just living for yourself, without Him. In all this, He chose you. What do you call this? Amazing love!!! This is His grace. But we do not stay there; we move on! We've been revived, changed! We're pressing forward. In the process, those things that do not belong will be shaken off.

The Creator's breath is in you. He breathed into you His breath of life so that you may live! He desires that we continually change and progress, moving forward. When true transformation comes, a heart change takes place. A heart of humility is there. Don't ever forget what God has done for you. He delivered you from the bondage of sin and death.

Psalm 23:1 says, *"The Lord is my shepherd, I shall not want [or lack]."* When He truly becomes your shepherd, you will not lack! He desires to be your shepherd. Why? So He may fulfill the promise of His Word in your life. He loves you enough to cause the shaking in your life so that you might not be separated or hindered from receiving His best for you. He has so many great and mighty things prepared for you that you have not even considered yet. But it is His desire to show them to you.[34]

God is able to do exceedingly abundantly above all that we ask or think, according to the power that works in us.[35] The power of the gift of the Holy Spirit in us gives us the ability

---

[33] Ephesians 2:10
[34] Jeremiah 33:3
[35] Ephesians 3:20

to receive all that He has for us. He teaches us and gives us understanding of the Scriptures, enabling us to obey the Lord.

The enemy of your soul will try to stop or hinder you from receiving this gift that our God has for you, because without it, you will be limited in God's revelation of His Word, *"do not forbid to speak with tongues."* [36]

The account of the Day of Pentecost in Acts chapter 2 speaks of how the 120 people *"...were, all filled with the Holy Spirit and began to speak with other tongues, as the Spirit gave them utterance."* Scripture tells us that *"...signs will follow those who believe, they shall speak with new tongues."* [37]

The gift of the baptism of the Holy Spirit with the evidence of speaking in tongues has power. Jesus said that it does. It allows the believer to pray perfectly in tune with God. It stops the working of the enemy and paves the way for you in the path of righteousness.

It is ironic that at one time, Navajo children were forbidden to speak their native language in the boarding schools to which they were shipped off in an attempt to Americanize them. Then, years later, the same language they had been forbidden to speak was a powerful tool to help win the war against America's enemy.

The enemy will try to take what belongs to you. He will try to rob you of your gifts—if you allow him to.

We're living in a day when the enemy is coming in like a flood and we, the church, are to lift up the standard of the Word of God. The Word is exalted when the people of God consistently demonstrate what they believe through how they live. This happens only one way: by the transformation of heart

---

[36] 1 Corinthians 14:39
[37] Acts 1:8

41

and mind and by living in surrender to Christ, who is the Word of God.

By standing in the righteousness that Christ clothes us with and by exercising the authority given to us by Him, the enemy's destructive plans are stopped as we lift up His Word in prayer.

God warned Noah that the flood was coming and told him to prepare by building an ark so his family and humanity would be saved.

Creator God is speaking to the church even this day, telling His people to prepare and to build an "Ark" of safety in Him so that we might have a safe place of refuge from the things that are coming upon the earth.

Chapter 4

THE ARK

"And God said to Noah, "The end of all flesh has come before Me, for the earth is filled with violence through them; and behold, I will destroy them with the earth. Make yourself an ark of gopherwood; make rooms in the ark, and cover it inside and outside with pitch. And this is how you shall make it: The length of the ark shall be three hundred cubits, its width fifty cubits, and its height thirty cubits. You shall make a window for the ark, and you shall finish it to a cubit from above; and set the door of the ark in its side. You shall make it with lower, second, and third decks."

—Genesis 6:13–16

In September of 1996, as we were in worship at the church we attended, I saw on the platform an ark like the one Noah built. It was a vision from the Spirit in my heart.

Then in November, on the seventh day of 2003, I was awakened at 3:12 in the morning. This is what I heard: "This is as the day of Noah. Build an ark. This is a place of protection

43

and refuge. I am dealing with families and this is a time of repentance and change, a turning point!

God is preparing us to go into the ark. What is the ark? It is a symbol of Christ, a refuge for God's people saved from judgment. It is also a place of deliverance, safety, and protection. It is a secure place.

The Spirit spoke to me just as the Lord spoke to Noah. Noah warned his family. The time for change had come and the process of preparation had to begin in order for God's people to be ready to enter the ark.

> *"By faith Noah, being divinely warned of things not yet seen, moved with godly fear, prepared an ark for the saving of his household, by which he condemned the world and became heir of the righteousness which is according to faith."*
>
> *—Hebrews 11:7*

As I lay in my bed on that morning of visitation, I pondered the vision I saw seven years earlier in 1996. I began to realize that the ark represented the true church and the ministry that He has called the Body of Christ to be a part of.

We are building the ark. God is giving us specific instructions. God is a specific God. He knows what is best for each and every one of us.

Noah was given specific instructions. God is preparing the church to be ready and to come into its place, which is living in His presence. It is in His presence that there is protection. His presence is a safe and secure place!

Psalm 91 describes a place of refuge and safety in God that has been prepared for us in much the same way as the ark was prepared for Noah. Psalm 91 reveals how the Creator's love, provision, and strength are directed toward those who habitually choose to obediently position themselves in the secret place of the prayer closet. It brings us under the protection of His love, authority, and provision. It's very encouraging as you begin to understand the depths of it.

No one can go under the secret place of the most high God and not change. Change comes under the secret place, a place that many are not aware of. It is a secret place of God's protection. This place is revealed by our Creator to the obedient of heart. It can be any place where the seeker of God is able to shut out the distractions of everyday life and have fellowship only with Him.

In 1999, a prophetic word was spoken by the Spirit. "The church is going to go through a spiritual wilderness before it enters the Promised Land." The spiritual always precedes the natural. Canaan is called the sanctuary, a safe place. For the children of Israel, the wilderness journey experience was outside of the Promised Land, where God taught them to rely on His leadership by the cloud of His presence and also to trust in His provision. God is leading the church by His Holy Spirit in much the same way today. We are to learn to obey the leading of His Holy Spirit and to trust in His faithfulness of provision. The church (the body of Christ, not a building, nor even a denomination), moving in unity, then becomes a sanctuary, a place of true worship, spirit to Spirit, a sacred, holy place, a place of refuge. A refuge is a place of shelter or protection from danger or trouble, a place of safety. From this place, God will cause His people to enter the Promised Land and to possess the gates of the enemy and every promise of blessing.

This sounds like the preparation of, and resulting safety of the ark. Noah's ark was where the presence of God dwelled.

> *"God said to Noah, I intend to make an end of all flesh,*
> *for through men the land is filled with violence; and*
> *behold, I will destroy them and the land. Make yourself*
> *an ark of gopher or cypress wood; make in it rooms*
> *(stalls, pens, coops, nests, cages, and compartments) and*
> *cover it inside and out with pitch (bitumen). And this*
> *is the way you are to make it: the length of the ark shall*
> *be 300 cubits, its breadth 50 cubits, and its height 30*
> *cubits [that is, 450 ft. x 75 ft. x 45 ft.]. You shall make*
> *a roof or window [a place for light] for the ark and finish*
> *it to a cubit [at least 18 inches] above—and the door of*
> *the ark you shall put in the side of it; and you shall make*
> *it with lower, second, and third stories."*
>
>

Genesis 6:13 – 16 Amplified Bible
>

God gave Noah detailed instructions. He told him to cover the ark with pitch inside and out. Pitch is Bitumen. Bitumen is a natural substance similar to asphalt used as a sealer, like cement and mortar.

God spoke to Noah and told him in detail what to use. Why was He so specific? Because he knew this substance had the strength to hold the ark together for what it was going to go through.

It is the same for us as it is for the church. God has provided us specific, detailed information. He knows what is coming down the road and what will be needed for us to succeed. He wants to protect us! God has given His church everything we need to excel, but the church can only be fully successful if we follow the specific instructions given.

Noah heeded the voice of the Lord because he was completely submitted to Him. The result was that he and all his family were saved.

There is now great concern for the present church generation. People have lost sight of the absolute necessity of adhering to the moral excellence of *all* of God's Word while at the same time understanding that this can only be accomplished by relying on His ability.

There is immeasurable value in the divine help that comes to us in the blessing of God and His power when we get past the elementary stages of spiritual development. It's time for mature believers to thrive on the meat, i.e., the deeper principles of the Word, in order to do the works of Christ.

Unfortunately, the fact of the matter is that this generation is in a place of summation of blessing, meaning that the church at large, without applying biblical principles, has come to the conclusion that they are blessed by God.

Yes, it is and has always been God's will from the very beginning for His people to live under "the blessing." He wants us to truly overflow with His provision in our lives so that we can be a blessing to others in every way possible. He has declared His desire that we should be the head, not the tail, only above and not beneath, [38] blessed in the city and blessed in the field.[39]

The prophetic Word of the Lord is wonderful, but that's not all there is. Success in daily living comes from diligent application of the principles of God's Word in our lives. But the Word of God must also be balanced with the Holy Spirit's guiding and teaching us those principles. Christians must be balanced by what the Word and the Spirit each instruct for their lives. On the one hand, the Bible tells us to "b*e diligent to present yourself approved to God, a worker who does not need to be*

---

[38] Deuteronomy 28:13
[39] Deuteronomy 28:3

ashamed, rightly dividing the word of truth.'[40] Scripture also tells us
that the Holy Spirit *"…will guide you into all truth; for He will not
speak on His own authority, but whatever He hears He will speak; and
He will tell you things to come.'*[41]

We need to be instructed in the Word by the Holy Spirit
for proper application of its principles. We so often enter into a
spiritual wilderness before entering the Promised Land.

The Navajo people endured the grueling Long Walk. It was
a wilderness journey that was spiritual as well as physical. Yes,
many died along the way. But the entire experience brought the
people to a place of crying out to Creator God. They learned,
once again, how to follow the Spirit of God, and they ended up
back on the very land God had sovereignly appointed to them.
God answered while they were in the midst of their wilderness
trial and delivered them back to their ancestral home.

Many are the trials in the life of a believer. Yet even when
it seems we're all alone, in the middle of a place where no man
has been before, we're not. God is ever faithful and will bring us
through to safety.[42] As we also follow the guidance of the Spirit,
we find our divinely appointed place or home in the world, in
the body of Christ.

Many of the Code Talkers were raised on the reservation.
They grew up in a house called a hogan. The Navajo word
hogan is literally translated as "place home." It combines the
meanings of home and of a sense of place. Often built of logs
and earth-covered, the Hogan provides a shelter against spring
winds, summer heat, and winter cold. This traditional Navajo
house is eight-sided or round, with one large room twenty feet
across, and benches and storage spaces lining the walls. The

---

[40] 2 Timothy 2:15
[41] John 16:13
[42] Psalm 34:19

floor is made of hard-packed dirt. It is warm in winter and cool in summer. The stove or fireplace sits in the center of the room and burns the central fire, which represents the North Star as an unmoving point of reference around which daily life revolves. The door of the Hogan always faces east to catch the rising sun, so that the Navajo can begin each day by greeting the light of the rising sun.

Building a Hogan is much more than simply providing a shelter. It is a way to make sense of the world, to live in harmony with the cycles and forces affecting all life. The Navajo ceremonial tradition of conducting "The Blessing Way" begins with songs detailing the plan and method of construction. These songs remind the people to build a place that will radiate beauty. Every structural detail, from pole to doorway, corresponds to a wider worldview layered with meaning.

God gave the Navajo specific instructions for building this place of protection. God provides each and every one of us with instructions and directions for building our lives on a solid foundation that will withstand the storms of life and the test of time (Luke 6:46–49).

If the Navajo people had not followed the wisdom of instruction given to them by their Creator, they would not have had the same degree of protection from the elements and understanding of their place in the world that a Hogan provides. Every material supplied had meaning and purpose; for example, the logs that form the walls of the hogan are joined together to represent the strong bond between a husband and a wife.

According to Ephesians 4:16, God instructs us that the Body of Christ is intended to be "*...joined and knit together by what every joint supplies, according to the effective working by which every part does its share, causes growth of the body for the edifying of itself in love.*" By using the means God has provided every believer to follow

His detailed instructions, the meaning, value, and purpose of living are made known to us.

The Hogan is a miniature universe. When a ceremony is conducted in the hogan, everything comes together. The people are set in place in the natural order of things. The dome roof represents the sky and the floor is the earth. The earth reminds the Navajo of who they are and where they came from: their bodies are made of dust, and to dust they return. Within the order of the hogan there is great love, and there is healing. In this place, health, prosperity, and a long, fulfilling life become possible. When you are touching earth, there is healing and love.

The concept of the Hogan teaches us about our home and also our place in the universe. The principle of divine order that is at work in the home and in the outer universe is the same principle at work within us because God is *"...upholding all things by the **word of his power.**"*[43]

Instruction is knowledge or information imparted as an act of teaching. God wants information imparted to us by His Word and confirmed by His Spirit within in us.

Hogans are still an important part of Navajo life today. Even people who don't live in hogans often build them for use in ceremonies because it reminds them of values important to their culture.

When God gave specific instruction to Noah for the building of the ark, it was an act of teaching. The Creator taught the Navajo to build the Hogan that would be their place of home, a place where they would dwell and worship Him. There they would meet with Creator in prayer to receive instruction and knowledge from Him.

---

[43] Hebrews 1:3

The Bible says, *"Noah walked with God."*[44] He obeyed God and lived according to what pleased God.

He was a righteous man. Therefore God taught him how to build a place of refuge and safety. The *"...LORD said to Noah, 'Come into the ark, you and all your household, because I have seen that you are righteous before Me in this generation.'"*[45]

The word righteous in this passage speaks of *"...one who is right, just, clear, clean, righteous; a person who is characterized by fairness, integrity and justice in his dealings. Being righteous brings a person light and gladness"* (Strong's Concordance, Strong's Number 6662). It is the righteous who shall live by his faith.[46]

People who live in the presence of God have fixed principles. They rule their own hearts and guide their thoughts and emotions. We must be a people who live by principle rather than being moved by passion alone. A principle is an accepted or professed rule of action or conduct. It is understanding that will bring about the blessing in your life.[47]

There are powerful teachings that will prepare you for life. We must not have a form of godliness or deny His power. Many neglect the rest of what 2 Timothy 3:5 tells us: *"And from such people turn away."* Some are still hanging around with people who deny His power and in doing so, their faith is diminished or degraded.

We must speak and walk in faith in order that we may place a demand on God's faithfulness to His Word, and therefore make a withdrawal from the richness of the account in Christ that is made available to each of us. We are to be prepared,

---

[44] Genesis 6:9
[45] Genesis 7:1
[46] Habakkuk 2:4
[47] Genesis 1:28

made ready in advance, built up in faith to be equipped to make a withdrawal. Some cannot make a significant withdrawal because there is not enough faith in them to be able to see or grasp the spiritual reality of God's covenant promises. You cannot wait until the storm comes to build the ark. You cannot wait to get the Word. You must be ready to speak the Word to yourself and get out of the boat and walk on the water.

If you do not continually deposit the Word into your spirit, you will have no substance to withdraw, because faith is giving substance to what you are confident of and expect to take place, according to the Word of God. Then you will operate in the negative, or in the red, when the storms of life come. This causes hearts to become overwhelmed by fear and doubt. This is why Jesus was constantly teaching life lessons of the spoken Word!

Let him that has an ear hear what the Spirit is saying:[48] "Hear!"

It's time, church! It's time to mature in the Word! There is a place where we mature in the Word, and it is in the Ark!

The same conditions and events that were present in the days of Noah are present now! God said to Noah, *"The end of all flesh has come before Me, for the earth is filled with violence through them; and behold, I will destroy them with the earth ..."* (Genesis 6:13). This violence God speaks of is acting with and characterized by uncontrolled, unrestrained force.

God wants you and me to be prepared and ready!

Jesus spoke of this when He said, *"But of that day and hour no one knows, not even the angels of heaven, but My Father only. But as the days of Noah were, so also will the coming of the Son of Man be. For as in the days before the flood, they were eating and drinking, marrying and giving in marriage, until the day that Noah entered the ark ..."* (Matthew 24:36–38).

---

[48] Revelation 2:7

In the vision that I saw back in September 1996, the ark had three levels. The lower level was full of lazy Christians; those who did not spend time with the Lord, that is, they spent no time praying or studying the Word. These people were of the "dead" church spoken of in Revelation 3:1–6, those who have a form of godliness by being in church every Sunday or busying themselves with religious activities.

The people in the middle level of the ark were "lukewarm Christians," the kind spoken of in Revelation 3:15–19. The lukewarm Christians were compromising and carnal, having given themselves over to the pleasures of and appetites for worldly things. Sin was condoned. They were eating, drinking, marrying, and giving in marriage, as in the day of Noah.[49] They were unaware that their destruction was upon them. This level consisted of three quarters of the amount of people in the lower level.

The third and highest level in the ark was appointed to the faithful church spoken of in Revelation 3:7–13. It had very few people in it. These were ones who spent quality time with God, being obedient seekers of Him. They were discerning, sober, alert, cautious, watchful, and awake. They were the elect who knew and obeyed His voice.

Today, many people occupy the lower and middle levels. They are the church that is either dead or lukewarm. For the most part, these people are in this condition because they have dismissed prayer in favor of other, more "entertaining" activities.

The birth of the Christian church is described in the book of Acts. In it, we see an awesome move of the Holy Spirit of God. Why? Because it was birthed out of prayer.

---

[49] Matthew 24:38

Every great revival in church history has been birthed out of prayer. Someone somewhere labored in the prayer closet to cause the Spirit of God to break forth.

By the end of the book of Acts, you see prayer stop; the church had stopped praying.

In the third chapter of Revelation, we read about three churches: the dead church, the faithful church, and the lukewarm church. As I studied my vision of the ark, I came to understand that the lower level was the dead church. They have a name and they are physically alive, but in reality, they are spiritually dead.

Outward appearances or works do not always characterize a right condition of heart, but a right condition of heart produces good works.

The second level of the ark, the lukewarm church, had works but they were neither cold nor hot. They had become rich and wealthy and said, "...I am rich and have need of nothing ...." And yet, they did not know they are wretched, miserable, poor, blind, and naked in the eyes of the Lord.

Jesus calls His people to be fully separated from the world's values system and to be totally committed to Him. The gauge of success for the believer is the measuring rod of God rather than the world's social and financial standards. When the Christian understands God's view from the eternal, the present comes into proper perspective.

We are not to adopt the world's way of thinking or its standards of behavior. We are not to value worldly success or to trust in worldly wealth. We should recognize that worldly assets have no spiritual or heavenly value.

The third level is the faithful church which is holy and true.

"'He who has the key of David, He who opens and no one shuts, and shuts and no one opens': 'I know your works. See, I have set before you an open door, and no one can shut it; ...'"

—Revelation 3:7–8

He who overcomes, I will make him a pillar in the temple of my God ... He who has an ear, let him hear what the Spirit says to the churches" (Revelation 3:12–13). He knows the works of the faithful church. It is the people of the faithful church that overcome and He makes them pillars in the temple.

The wise believer makes time to hear with a spiritual ear what the Spirit is saying to the church. This is as critical today as it was in the first century. One who hears and follows the voice of the Holy Spirit need not fear deception, which leads to apostasy.

We are the church. The church has been given precise, clear instructions and direction regarding God's plan. It is through prayer that we can hear, in our own spirit, what the Spirit of God is speaking.

The church in Ephesus had left its first love. Laodicea had become lukewarm. Why? Because they had abandoned prayer and their dependence on God. Consequently, their hearts turned cold.

It is important you know in your heart that your first place is to have a prayer life and your time in the Word. The only way you can have a vital, healthy relationship with God is to have these elements operating in your life on a continual basis!

Long before they ever became Marines, the Code Talkers were taught to pray. They had to be sensitive to the creator's direction. They had to abide by what they were taught by their parents. They may not have known the Word as fully as many of us know it today, but they had a relationship with God based on what they did know and understand. Many of the parents of these young men knew their God, the Creator!

We have a responsibility of duty to pray! Since the fall of man through Adam, God has never moved on the earth without doing it through relationship with man. Mankind has earthly license for heavenly interference.

God desires to see His people saved and protected.

Noah built the ark according to all that God commanded him. Noah didn't build the Ark to satisfy himself. He didn't usurp authority. He did not argue with God or refuse and tell God "No, I want to do it *my* way!" Remember, Noah built the ark according to all that God commanded (Genesis 6:22).

Noah found grace and favor with God and saved the human race through his faithfulness and obedience. Noah was righteous before God in his generation.

The ark is also symbolic of Christ, who is the refuge of His people from judgment of sin. Did the judgment come on Noah, his wife or his family? No! The Ark saved them from it. It was their place of safety and refuge.

Life brings with it major events. There are floods we all go through both good and bad. If you haven't yet experienced a flood, know that it's coming! It could be a flood of overwhelming adversity, or perhaps an abundance of something you are not able to handle in a healthy way, i.e., in your own wisdom and strength. Or, it could even be a flood of something supernatural.

When a person receives the baptism of the Holy Spirit there is a flood in their spirit by the supernatural working of God.

The night I received the baptism of the Holy Spirit with the evidence of speaking in tongues, a flood swept over my inner spirit man. I was on the floor laughing as if I were drunk and I spoke in tongues for hours as waves of God's love, joy, and peace swept over me. Even after I went home, I continued like that for the next three days.

In both the natural and the spiritual realms, God wants us to be prepared and ready! He desires us to know how to properly deal with and handle the issues of living. He desires for us to stay in the Ark. In the Ark, in Christ, there is safety and protection to be found.

You may ask, "Protection against what?" Protection from the floods that come as a result of the operations and effects of this fallen world's system that war against our walk with the Lord.

It was in the Ark, the place of God's positioning for him, that Noah was able to fulfill what God called him to do.

Church! There is an Ark and it's called the presence of God, the place of safety and protection.

On the third and highest level of the Ark is where we can live close to Him, and in His very presence! It's in that place we hear Him clearly and are imparted to by Him. It's in the Ark of His presence that we have life and remain spiritually alive and healthy.

God's Word tells us that only the righteous, Noah, and those who were with him remained alive.[50]

Noah went into the Ark as God commanded him, *"and the Lord shut him in."*[51] Notice that the Lord shut him in; it was God's doing. It was God's decision! Noah didn't shut the door; the Lord shut the door as He chose. This was the timing of God!

God tests us. He tests our faith and obedience. Most often, we are given multiple opportunities to fulfill His will for His calling upon our lives. Nevertheless, in His loving wisdom, God shuts the door of opportunity when He chooses. God looks at

---

[50] Genesis 7:23

[51] Genesis 7:16

our hearts, our motives, our attitudes, our ambitions, and our actions.

Church, we are on a timetable, just as Noah was on a timetable.

We are walking in the timing of the Lord. If we declare we are functioning in our lives according to His plan and purpose, then we must make sure we are also in His timing! God can do anything. He can shut the door whenever He chooses. I surely don't want Him to shut the door until I have fulfilled my obedience to His voice.

When Noah had completed all his instructions in obeying the voice of the Lord, God spoke to him again, saying, *"Go out of the ark, you and your wife, and your sons and your sons' wives with you. Bring out with you every living thing of all flesh that is with you: birds and cattle and every creeping thing that creeps on the earth, so that they may abound on the earth, and be fruitful and multiply on the earth"* (Genesis 8:15–17).

Noah was obedient to God. He completed his task after having gone through a season of preparation.

To everything there is a season and time. When God created heaven and earth, it was a completed work. When He had finished everything He planned to do, He set time as we know it in motion. He started the clock, if you will.

He set the time for the Navajo Code Talkers. He created the language and also that point in time during WWII when their language would be used to benefit our nation.

God spoke to Noah, reasserting the blessing, His desire, and His plan for mankind, just as He had spoken to the first man, Adam, when He said, *"...Be fruitful and multiply; fill the earth ...."*[52]

When we hear God's instructions and complete the task at hand, the Lord will then lead us to the next one. From

---

[52] Genesis 1:28

faith to faith, the righteousness of God is revealed in us from one obedience to the next. In this, we see tangible fruit and multiplication in our lives and in the Body of Christ on the earth.

The church is at a turning point. We are entering into a new season. Change is the order of the day. So much is at stake. We cannot afford to be caught unaware or unprepared.

The apostle Paul admonishes us even more as we recognize the approach of the day of the Lord. Paul writes, *"...concerning the times and the seasons, brethren, you have no need that I should write to you. For you, yourselves know perfectly that the day of the Lord so comes as a thief in the night. For when they say, 'Peace and safety!' then sudden destruction comes upon them, as labor pains upon a pregnant woman. And they shall not escape. But you, brethren, are not in darkness, so that this Day should overtake you as a thief. You are all sons of light and sons of the day. We are not of the night nor of darkness. Therefore let us not sleep, as others do, but let us watch and be sober (1 Thessalonians 5:1–6).*

The word "sober" is defined as being self-controlled.

God is preparing us to get into the Ark where we are alert, watchful, sober, cautious, and on guard. As seekers of God, the Lord would have us be ready and prepared so that He may move us to a higher level in the Ark of relationship with Him. It is in this place that we have intimate relationship with Him and it is this relationship that overcomes the religion of man!

Chapter 5

RELATIONSHIP OVERCOMES RELIGION

"Abide in Me, and I in you. As the branch cannot bear fruit of itself, unless it abides in the vine, neither can you, unless you abide in Me. 'I am the vine, you are the branches. He who abides in Me, and I in him, bears much fruit; for without Me you can do nothing.'"

—*John 15:4–5*

In the place of His presence, we create relationship. I have learned that the religion of men can take you to the door (to Christ) but will not allow you to experience the fullness of intimate relationship. Jesus rebuked the religious leaders of His day when He said, *". . .woe to you, scribes and Pharisees, hypocrites! For you shut up the kingdom of heaven against men; for you neither go in yourselves, nor do you allow those who are entering to go in."* (Matthew 23:13)

Some say, "Oh, I've been a Christian for many years." But Christian maturity does not come from the passage of time alone. What matters most is the amount of quality time spent in His presence and the council of His Word. One's rate of spiritual development is dependent upon this. New, hungry Christians often pass by older Christians—i.e., those who are religious, spiritually lazy, and not truly yielded—as though the older were standing by the side of the freeway watching the new ones go by.

God desires you to be prepared for His coming. He wants to fulfill every promise from the Bible and every prophetic word spoken over your life. He's provided for your entire being, body, soul, and spirit, to be complete in Him—and not just in part, in half-hearted obedience. [53] He requires a complete surrender of self will in preference to His will.

Too many people have the religious notion, "If I surrender all, I'll never get to have any fun or do anything I enjoy." But what we find, in practice, is that quite the opposite is true. Jesus said, *"If ye then, being evil, know how to give good gifts unto your children, how much more shall your Father which is in heaven give good things to them that ask him?"*[54] Surrender doesn't mean you can't live your life. When you make Jesus the priority of your life, the blessing of God will cause all grace to abound "...toward you, that you, always having all sufficiency in all *things*, may have an abundance for every good work."[55] He will make good on every promise that will cause your life to be rich in His goodness. He wants to be included in every part of your life.

God's instruction to every believer is to belong to a Bible-believing, Spirit-filled church. But our life must not be 'just' about going to church. First and foremost it's all about relationship with Him.

On the other hand, I've heard people say, "I don't need to go to church; it's about relationship." When you have true, intimate relationship, you're going to want to obey God and be in church to hear what the Spirit of God is saying to the Body

---

[53] 1 Thessalonians 5:23
[54] Matthew 7:11
[55] 2 Corinthians 9:8

of Christ. This is a critical element of the believer's spiritual health and life. The purpose of God's freely giving us all things that pertain to life and godliness in Christ is that we, in turn, will give freely as well.[56]

Often, religion means well, but makes the things of God harder than they need to be.

My Dad would always rise in the early morning, as taught by Navajo tradition. His ninety-six years of age testified of the strength of his belief that one who does this will live a long life.

Sometimes my father would pray with the *ta'a'didi'i'n*, or corn pollen that comes from the corn stalk. It is applied to the forehead in acknowledging oneself as being a holy child, part of the universe. In this you are offering prayers as a holy earth person. You are offering your prayer to the Creator, who is in the third spirit world. When one prays, they pray toward the east; this helps to clear one's thoughts so that the mind is ready for the day.

My grandparents recognized that many of their cultural beliefs were mysterious to white men. So also, in the natural, there is much about the things of God that is difficult if not impossible to know unless the understanding or revealing of it is communicated by the Spirit of God.

> *"But the natural man does not receive the things of the Spirit of God, for they are foolishness to him; nor can he know them, because they are spiritually discerned."*
> —1 *Corinthians 2:14*

Natural thinking is opposed to God. The human mind considers the things of the Spirit of God foolish because it cannot understand them. In futility, man has always tried to

---

[56] 2 Peter 1:3

put God in a neat mental box. However, there isn't a box big enough to house God the Creator. Neither is there one big enough to house the human spirit He created. God made us in His image and His likeness. Our God is a mysterious God.

When I was a young child, my mother would tell me, "Don't ever limit God. He can do great and mighty things that we cannot understand."

The Lord is ever preparing us to reach the place of destiny He has been leading us to. The church has been going through a process of preparation! What is preparation? It is the procedure of moving forward through which one prepares for the future beforehand, making ready a proper state of mind for service or duty. We are in preparation for a journey (traveling from one place to another, progressing from one stage to another), the journey to success.

I see God speaking to people individually in a clear, distinctive way. God is calling each believer to draw closer to Him. Why? In order that His people may possess the fullness of His promise of restoration and manifestation of His Kingdom by seeing it literally come to pass in their lives.

Each of us has special qualities. God created us to be different and unique with individual inward as well as outward features and characteristics. We are set apart as different, special, and precious to Him. He is calling at this time and this very hour for His people to prepare. The future of the church is bright and filled with hope for those who equip and position themselves to be a part of what He is doing on the earth.

> *"For I know the thoughts that I think toward you, says the LORD, thoughts of peace and not of evil, to give you a future and a hope."*
> —*Jeremiah 29:11*

The Lord has a plan for our future.

"A man's heart plans his way, but the Lord directs his steps."[57] See, church, the Holy Spirit who dwells in you. He wants to lead you and guide you and direct you in every way of living! But close, intimate relationship with Him is the only way this can happen.

God has given each of us a Word and a promise. Many of us have heard the prophetic or perhaps have been given a personal word of prophesy. A personal prophesy simply refers to a message spoken by the Holy Spirit through one person to another for their benefit. Many times, that Word is not completely new in the spirit and mind of the person it is spoken to. Rather, it confirms something about which God has already been dealing with them. In the light of the Word, we should prayerfully consider what is said.

In this closeness of healthy relationship with the Lord, it is crucial that we learn to hear and know His voice. Through quality time spent with Him in fellowship and study of Scripture, we are guided by His Spirit. In this way we follow the path of obedience to fulfillment of those things spoken into our individual lives.

Prophecy comes to us in part, just as the Word says.

"For we know in part and we prophesy in part."
—*1 Corinthians 13:9*

This means that, as true as that "part" may be, it does not give the whole picture. God is calling us to a special place for a certain time. It is sure to happen and bound to come. Some may ask, "When is this certain time?" Well, ask God; He will tell you. When a prophetic Word is given by the Holy Spirit it

---

[57] Proverbs 16:9

does not necessarily contain every detail of the whole picture. The reason for this is that it requires us to draw closer to Him to learn the rest. God wants us to learn that our dependence upon Him is to be ongoing.

There have been many prophesies spoken to the church, both as individuals and as the corporate body.

The Spirit of God is speaking corporately to the church for our nation. What happened to the days when we prayed for our nation as a church body? What happened to our Pledge of Allegiance to the United States of America, One nation under God? Allegiance is being loyal as citizen to one's government or as a subject to one's sovereign king.

All America's soldiers gave some and some gave all in the fight for our national freedoms and liberties. It was never ever fought in vain.

This is where the church is today. Christians take what they do in church too lightly. Their participation in religious activities has become a form of religion and often has the appearance of godliness but has no substance of power in it.

Whatever happened to the time when national leaders described America as a shining city on a hill? Naturally, this description originated with Jesus Christ. Yet our nation, once a shining flame of freedom, is now well on the road to becoming a fading ember of debt, hopelessness, discord, and defeat. But this does not have to continue.

Who, then, bears the primary responsibility for this predicament? I believe Christians do. Believers are called to be light and to reveal that light to the world in order to inspire the continuing presence of a shining city that truly cannot be hidden.

In the Sermon on the Mount, Jesus used the analogy that believers are both salt and light. Salt helps preserve what is precious and important while enhancing flavor. Similarly, the Christian witness should have a positive effect on every facet of life and culture. If salt loses its effect, Jesus said, it is good for nothing but to be trampled under the feet of men.

Surely everything sacred is being trampled under the feet of those who consider God to be unimportant or nonexistent. Faith in God, family values, and basic freedoms are being trampled by many who call themselves liberals, socialists, and activists.

Many stumble in darkness because they have been commanded to place the "light" in a prominent place, on a lampstand. They have actually diminished and even hidden their influence from the public by accepting religious labels, false comfort, compromise, and self-satisfaction. Light reveals the way to security and success while illuminating dangers and pitfalls. It's no small wonder we are in such trouble when salt and light fail to accomplish their divine assignment. Although it is true that these are the "last days," this does not justify a lack of commitment and action. Paul the apostle, the disciples, and New Testament Christians believed, even then, that they were living in the last days.

Nevertheless, they did not rest. They faithfully began a spiritual revolution, turning their upside-down world right side up. They were courageous, bold, and fearless as uncompromising witnesses. Moved to action by the Spirit of God that was overflowing from them, they were in control of every area of their lives.

Paul tearfully warned the people day and night, calling them to repentance. His challenge to fight the good fight of faith as a good soldier of Christ is extended to every true believer today. We have been appointed to be witnesses until He comes. Now is the time to stir ourselves up in the Spirit, our thinking renewed to God's truth, holding up that truth above every circumstance contrary to it, wielding the Word of God as a sword, and going out to win the battle against the devil and the godless, self-serving, and vain promises of mortal men.

This is our time, our day of visitation! When you know who you are in Christ, there is a light that comes out of you and blinds the devil. In order for us to properly respond to this appointed time, we must draw closer to Him! We are to be like the sons of Issachar, who understood the times and had knowledge revealed to them so that they would know what to do, having eyes to see the enemy.

The young Code Talkers knew the time they were in. They came to realize that if they did not have ears to hear when the enemy was coming, they would fail their mission and die. They understood they were to be prepared, ready at all times. These warriors knew their hope of success lay in sticking with the battle plan given to them by their commander. Likewise, we have been given commands by Jesus the Great Commander. Obedience and victory do not come without their own price.

This is the day of visitation for the Body of Christ. For all who would seek and heed Him, the opportunity to be ready has been graciously offered. We are to be alert and sober-minded so that we do not miss this appointed time.

The children of Israel missed their day of visitation. Because of the hardness of their hearts, they could not hear what Jesus was really telling them. The greatness of God had been manifested in the Son of Man in order that the Jews might recognize the fulfillment of literally hundreds of prophesies foretelling the coming of the Kingdom of God on the earth. This greatly grieved the heart of God.

As Jesus "...drew near, He saw the city and wept over it ..."[58]

---

[58] Luke 19:41

He wept audibly, which means loud enough to be heard. He wept! Why would He do this? He wept because they had missed their time of visitation. They were not prepared.

In the Amplified version Luke 19:42 Jesus exclaims "... Would that you had known personally, even at least in this your day ..." Your day is the day of your power, the day that God has prepared for you.

Jesus mourned because they were not prepared or even able to recognize Him as the fulfillment of the covenant blessing of God. They could have been equipped and ready for the difficult things that were to come. They could have been prepared for the days when calamity, oppression, and destruction would surround them. They could have had all of heaven's resources on hand to deal with whatever happened.

He's saying "I showed up to answer every prayer that you prayed and to bring to pass every dream that you've ever had. A time is coming upon you when your enemies will throw up a bank (with pointed stakes) about you and surround you and shut you in on every side."[59]

All of this "...*because you did not come progressively to recognize and know and understand [from observation and experience] the time of your visitation.*" [60] Visitation is when God visits you and shows Himself gracious toward you.

This is our time, church! I'm determined that by God's grace I'm not going to miss my day of visitation. Will you? Start with yourself and then unite as the corporate Body of Christ with others everywhere who also have this same mindset. I am determined to not miss His goodness! I believe I will not miss His blessings.

---

[59] Luke 19:42 Amplified Bible
[60] Luke 19:44b Amplified Bible

Stand, rise as that great and mighty warrior! It's ready to happen! God wants to raise up more voices, not just echoes. It's here! Our time is here and now! There is a stirring, an urgency! There is an excitement, an anticipation! The trumpet is blowing; make ready and gather together!

Decide that you will have an ear to hear what the Spirit is saying. Those who do not prepare will not hear. Those who have not drawn close to the Lord in intimacy of relationship with Him cannot see or discern what is at hand!

Church! It's possible that your day of visitation can come and go, right in front of you, and you won't even know it. How could this happen? By you not being prepared. God desires that we be ready at all times. Our hearts are to always be open and receptive to His voice, humbling ourselves, always positioned in an attitude of repentance.

The day of visitation is *NOW*, church! The time of harvest is here! Great things are about to happen. Jesus is coming! He's coming for the true church, a Holy church, without spot or wrinkle.

> *"For thus says the High and Lofty One who inhabits*
> *eternity, whose name is Holy:*
> *"I dwell in the high and holy place, with him who has a*
> *contrite (sincere) and humble spirit, to revive the spirit of*
> *the humble, and to revive the heart of the contrite ones."*
> *—Isaiah 57:15*

One who is humble in spirit is meek, patient, or docile, as under provocation from others, teachable. Meekness is not weakness, but absolute power under perfect control.

The church must be teachable. Those who have a humble and contrite, or self-crushed spirit, are those who can receive the instruction of the Lord; it's the one who invites and allows God to change him, the one who walks in humility before Him, the one who submits to Him, the one who obeys Him. These are of great value to the Lord.[61]

When you come to that place of submission to and complete dependence upon Him, you experience the blessing; you experience favor! It's sad to say, but most Christians don't live in the favor of God. Why? Because they live in the place called "familiar." They choose to remain in the place that's comfortable to them. There is no change! Too many are still living at the same level of undeveloped faith and obedience at which they were five, ten, or twenty years ago. There is no growth or advancement in their walk with God. The carnal attitudes of pride and self-centeredness still sit on the throne of their lives!

Obey God with the expectation that He will help you when you choose the way of His Word. Don't ever forget what Christ has done for you! He has brought us out of the darkness of sin's deception and into the light of the truth of His Word.

The Sprit of God is calling and wooing people to the place of personal intimacy. Relationship overcomes religion. Close relationship with God in Christ overcomes the deceit of man's religion. Many churches today have large crowds of people attending services and participating in all sorts of religious activities. Yet too many have only heard about Jesus. They don't know for themselves who He really is.

It is the power of His grace working in you that will bring you into true relationship.

As previously mentioned, God spoke a defining word to me just before the start of the Sunday-morning service back in

---

[61] Psalm 51:17

September, 2009. Our church building is small. Built in 1937, it's located at the birthplace of the city. The sanctuary seats around sixty people comfortably. It's been restored and looks like an older chapel.

Intercessory prayer had just ended and as the service was ready to start. Worship music was playing. I continued to pray as people came in and filled up the church. Aware that many people were coming in, I turned around. And when I did, this is what I heard in my spirit: "Would you rather have 'this' or My power?" I began to weep and, with a shaking and quivering in my voice, I answered, "Your power." And He said, "What do you see in a circus?" I remember the thought that came to me: "A circus in the church?"

I thought about this for a moment, and then these words came out of my own mouth as if the Spirit of the Lord were speaking through me: "There are groups of people coming in and out, cliques, tricks, games, and entertainment. This is in the church."

My husband and I had begun the ministry in 2004 with the determination that, by the grace of God, we would not be religious, but rather, always be sensitive and yielded to the heart of God in trust of whatever He would have us to do. Interestingly enough, I recognized that many of the people in the church were coming more out of self-interest and not from a true desire to reverence and worship God. We believed we could help them through God's love, the power of the Holy Spirit, and the truth of God's Word.

This event dramatically changed my perception of the true condition of the church as a whole.

Choosing His power was the most profound ministry decision I had made up to that point. I realized I had made the biggest decision in my life to move from a religious form to a place of focusing on true relationship with the Lord.

This was a revelation about what has become of the church in general and what we're up against (the circus in the church) which has become the expectation of those attending.

I believe that there are many churches today that do not recognize this spirit of religion, this form of godliness that has crept into the church. Many leaders are not even aware that this is the case. To others, it is known, but they have chosen to ignore it for reasons of their own.

Since that day, the ministry we were entrusted to has made a complete U-turn. As prayer began to increase, the presence and power of God increased as well. We began to discern and understand at a deeper level the critical importance of staying focused on the vision and plan for the ministry that has been given to us.

When the presence and power of God comes in the church it always requires change. Darkness and the works of the enemy that hinder the work of God are exposed. It is then the responsibility of those in authority to deal with it according to the Word and the leading of the Holy Spirit.

When we ministered the Word of Truth under the anointing of God, hidden things began to be revealed. There was no condemnation or finger-pointing but simply the Holy Spirit working through truth in the hearts of people. But the call for genuine commitment and consecration to the will and purposes of God caused many to become uncomfortable because they were not willing to yield. The conviction for change became so strong that those who refused to yield to the Spirit couldn't handle it. Accordingly, there began to be fewer people in the church. In the end, there was a true transformation that took place in all of us and in the ministry as a whole. What we found was that transformation does not necessarily mean you will end up with a lot of people. Very often, the more people there are, the more difficult it is to have true agreement and unity.

There are sizable churches that many times have the least transformation. The presence of a large church in a community doesn't necessarily mean that it is making a spiritual impact.

It's not really about how many people come together. It's about walking in God-given dominion. Dominion is the power to govern, sovereign authority (*Random House Webster's College Dictionary*).

The young native Code Talkers had to adopt a changed mindset. It was critical for their thoughts to aligned with true authority: their commander, the one who had the plan and the strategy.

Likewise, it is critical for believers to have a transformed mindset. We must come under God's authority and into agreement with His way, His plan, and His strategy. We must fall into formation with the great planner, our Creator. The church must have a change in its thinking. Thinking is renewed by the Word of God.

When we are first introduced to other pastors, the number one thing we are asked first is, "How big is your church?" This seems to be the immediate standard by which pastors measure their ministerial success among each other. The real truth of the matter is that how many people a church has is not as important as how much spiritual influence is being brought to bear by the working of the ministry of that church. Men tend to set the standard of their own success by how many resources can be gathered, whether they are people, finances, materials, etc.

Without question, the wielding of these things signals power and influence. However, it's possible for a church to have thousands of members, tremendous financial strength, and mega resources, but still have little to no spiritual influence.

God uses a different standard. He measures success on a case-by-case basis. He determines success on the basis of our obedience to His specific commands to leadership and the people who follow that leadership based on their relationship with Him.

A prominent aspect of our culture today is entertainment. If people are not entertained, they become bored and disengaged. This mindset has crept into the church to the point that entertainment has become the main focus. It seems the church has lost sight of its true purpose. The apostle Paul identified that the purpose of the church is "...to make all see what *is* the fellowship of the mystery, which from the beginning of the ages has been hidden in God who created all things through Jesus Christ; to the intent that now the manifold wisdom of God might be made known by the church to the principalities and powers in the heavenly *places.* ..."[62]

In the time of the Judges, the Midianites and the people of the east came to war against the people of Israel with an army so large the soldiers in it couldn't be counted. Gideon assembled an army of 32,000 men to fight for Israel and the Lord said, *"The people who are with you are too many for Me to give the Midianites into their hands, lest Israel claim glory for itself against Me, saying, 'My own hand has saved me.'"*[63]

This is just like the church claiming the glory of accomplishment by the hand of its own resourcefulness in organization and self-sufficiency. The Lord wanted to reveal Himself to the people of Israel by using only 300 men to save Israel, to show them His power!

---

[62] Ephesians 3:10
[63] Judges 7:2

The Lord also said to Gideon, *"proclaim in the hearing of the people, saying, 'Whoever is fearful and afraid, let him turn and depart at once from Mount Gilead.'" And twenty-two thousand of the people returned, and ten thousand remained."*[64]

There are many fearful people in the church. They are afraid to pay the cost, "to let go and let God," to submit themselves in faith to be tested beyond what they have known. They often disagree with the direction their faith walk with God is leading. But these fearful ones have not had a revelation of who they truly are in Christ.

Now that 10,000 men remained, the Lord said, *"The people are still too many; bring them down to the water, and I will test them."* (Judges 7:4)

"The number of those who lapped water by putting their hands to their mouths was 300 men. They were the ones who were able to watch for the enemy even as they put their hands to their mouths.

It was with this small band of 300 that the Lord delivered the entire nation of Israel.

Those who know who they are in Christ, those who trust in Him, those who are obedient, watchful, and alert, shall stand their ground and remain.

I would also say that there was unity within the 300 men. It would be a lot harder for 32,000 men to achieve unity. It might not take 32,000 to save a city. With the 300, there was power in Mount Gilead. But having such a small number of men made Gideon pretty nervous.

It would tend to make any leader nervous. It certainly made me nervous when I chose power over the quantity. But God caused Gideon to be built up in boldness and courage so that

---

[64] Judges 7:3

75

he would be able to follow His instructions faithfully and gain victory over his enemy.

Power is the principle requirement for total release! There is no real advancement against the enemy of God's people without His power in operation. This power is above every other power. The enemy cannot stop this!

The enemy could not stop the Code Talkers from carrying out the plan that was originated by those in authority. Their language had power in it. The enemy could not understand this. The code could not be broken!

Where there is true relationship with the Creator, there is divine power, true POWER!

God speaks to His true servants, *"Call to Me, and I will answer you, and show you great and mighty things, which you do not know."*[65]

When believers consistently call upon the Lord in prayer, relationship grows. We are the ones who complete the connection of true relationship with Him because God has already accomplished His part through the finished work of Christ. God promised the prophet Jeremiah that if he would call upon Him, He would answer and reveal profound and wonderful things that were not possible to know otherwise.

This word "mighty" in this passage is perhaps better rendered as "isolated" or "inaccessible" Only God can reveal these things to us. Only He can give us revelatory insight. This kind of insight has always been critical for a clear understanding of victorious spiritual warfare.

These things are privileged information that God makes known only to those who are functioning citizens of His Kingdom.

There is power in prayer. We are created to have that same power Jesus has. We are to believe the impossible. However, in

---

[65] Jeremiah 33:3

order to do that, a person must first see the invisible. Seeing into the invisible realm is a key to victorious praying; it involves discerning spiritual issues from God's viewpoint rather than man's, seeing the enemy's attack plan, and perceiving God's angelic strike force.

In sincere relationship with God, we come to know Him not only through His Word, but also even further by observation, investigation, reflection, and firsthand experience. An even greater level of knowing is that which comes through direct intimate contact.

On the battlefield, the Code Talkers would often see the enemy's attack plan unfolding before them. Regardless, they believed their Creator had a better plan and would bring them through because *"...the people who know their God shall be strong, and carry out great exploits."*[66]

Relationship of this kind is a life-giving intimacy as can be found in marriage. Applied spiritually, the intimacy of our prayer conceives and births blessings and victories.

God affirms this truth when He says, *"Trust in the LORD with all your heart, and lean not on your own understanding; In all your ways acknowledge Him, and He shall direct your paths."* [67]

God tells us that if we trust, being bold, confident, and secure in Him, holding to His ways of doing things, He promises to make our paths straight and right as He directs us toward fruitful, life-begetting endeavors.

The church is called to live a godly life. Godliness includes three elements: love, obedience, and unity. In living a godly life, we learn to see things like God sees them and to adopt His Word as our only standard. We are to commit ourselves to the unity of the church. But this can only come as our minds are

---

[66] Daniel 11:32

[67] Proverbs 3:5–6

renewed to the conclusion that absolute agreement in Word and witness of the Holy Spirit within our own spirit is the only way to have true unity and relationship with Him and with each other.[68]

In Jesus' final petition of prayer to the Father, He prays for the unity of all believers. He says, *"I do not pray for these alone, but also for those who will believe in Me through their word; that they all may be one, as You, Father, are in Me, and I in You; that they also may be one in Us, that the world may believe that You sent Me. And the glory which You gave Me I have given them, that they may be one just as We are one: I in them, and You in Me; that they may be made perfect in one, and that the world may know that You have sent Me, and have loved them as You have loved Me."* [69]

The oneness that Jesus requests is not so much organizational as spiritual unity of soul and spirit, individually as well as corporately. The Spirit of God is speaking this same Word to all churches, all ethnic groups, and all the nations of the world. Jesus redeems His people, His church, "…out of every tribe and tongue and people and nation." [70]

Back in August of 2005, my husband and I were praying. I saw a vision of west-coast Native American tribes walking toward the center of the United States. They were joined together, arm in arm, shoulder to shoulder, with all their regalia on. As I continued to pray, I asked the Lord, "What is this?" And this is what I heard: "The tribes of the west coast are headed to the middle part of America to reconcile with those tribes that have come to a place of repentance." I did not see anything else but a semicircle of west-coast tribes headed toward the east.

---

[68] 1 Corinthians 1:10
[69] John 17:20–23
[70] Revelation 5:9b

Two months later, we were at a church meeting on a reservation in Southern California. During the worship service, I saw a vision, just as I had a couple months previous. What I saw was the Native American tribes from the east coast heading toward the center of the United States. They were also joined together, arm in arm, shoulder to shoulder, dressed in their regalia. As we continued to worship, I saw all the tribes come together; the circle was complete.

It is written, *"It is He who sits above the circle of the earth."* [71] The eternal circle of covenant is complete when there is repentance and reconciliation to God and to each other. With this circle, He intervenes to restore.

For these last days, Native Americans are being positioned to be utilized by God in their spiritual role as they take their appointed place in the Body of Christ.

I believe God is raising up faithful believers for the end-time revival, much in the same way the young Navajo Code Talkers were raised up for the war in 1942.

God is calling the watchmen to sound the alarm when He says, *"Proclaim this among the nations: 'Prepare for war! Wake up the mighty men, let all the men of war draw near, let them come up.'"* [72]

There is a *"...noise of a multitude in the mountains like that of many people! A tumultuous noise of the kingdoms of nations gathered together! The Lord of hosts musters the army for battle."* [73]

A visitation of the power of God the likes of which the world has never known is at hand. A harvest on a scale we have never seen is about to happen! In some places it's happening already! The question then is, How is God going to do this? The answer is through the process of preparing and cleansing the hearts

---

[71] Isaiah 40:22a
[72] Joel 3:9
[73] Isaiah 13:4

and lives of those who make up the beloved Body of Christ, by allowing God's Spirit to have full freedom in us, His temple, His church. Becoming free demands a transformation of heart and mind. When the Spirit of God is manifest in the church, His people are empowered to change! Pride, selfishness, and fleshly lusts are dealt with. For "...*if anyone cleanses himself from the latter (dishonor), he will be a vessel for honor, sanctified and useful for the Master, prepared for every good work.*"[74]

As the people of the church prepare and sanctify themselves, set themselves apart from the influence of the world, and seek the Lord, they become vessels for honor and useful or profitable to the Master. The people of God have been given everything in Christ that is needed to accomplish the good work He has assigned His Body. Seek Him first, and then you will find true relationship with Him.

---

[74] 2 Timothy 2:21

Conclusion

IN THE END

"I am the Alpha and the Omega, the Beginning and the End, the First and the Last." [14] Blessed are those who do His commandments, that they may have the right to the tree of life, and may enter through the gates into the city. I am the Alpha and the Omega, the Beginning and the End, the First and the Last."[14] Blessed are those who do His commandments that they may have the right to the tree of life, and may enter through the gates into the city."
—Revelation 22:13–14

There is a strong, heartfelt cry in the Spirit for repentance and reconciliation. Reconciliation is the process by which God and man are brought together again. This is made possible through the blood of Jesus, which demonstrates the power of and the model for reconciliation.

As children of God and joint heirs with Jesus Christ, we are enjoined to follow the standard He left for us: to be reconciled to God and with each other as He reconciled us to Him. As we model His ministry of reconciliation, the world will be impacted."

God has appointed His church to make a difference in the earth. The only real impact that can be made is through lives lived in Christ, in His love. Tenderness of heart and uprightness of godly character in the people of God are sustained in a lifestyle of repentance and forgiveness. This is the demonstration of genuineness made to a world blind in heart and hardened to the gospel by religious hypocrisy.

Native Americans are coming to a place of reconciliation that is bringing them into agreement and harmony with other tribes and peoples with whom they have long had enmity. Repentance and forgiveness must start in the house of God before it can go outward.

The redemptive blood of Jesus was shed for every human being on this planet. God did not create us to have thousands of denominations (as if there were more than one Body of Christ). We are not given credit by God for belonging to a certain denomination. We must have a change of mind that comes by receiving the Word of God by faith in application.

Romans 12:1–2 commends us to present ourselves as a living sacrifice, holy to God. We must not conform to this world system of thinking and behaving, but be transformed by the renewing of our minds and be committed to the ideals of the Kingdom of God.

In order for this transformation to take place, there must be a surrender of the heart in repentance as we humble ourselves under the mighty hand of God. Repentance is a decision that results in a change of mind, which in turn leads to a change of purpose and direction.

> *"Repent therefore and be converted, that your sins may be blotted out, so that times of refreshing may come from the presence of the Lord,"*
>
> —Acts 3:19

The first call of the Kingdom is to repentance. From the outset of His ministry, "... Jesus began to preach and to say, "Repent, for the Kingdom of heaven is at hand."[75]

The Kingdom of heaven has arrived, church! The Kingdom is within us. The Spirit of our Creator lives within, enabling us to do what God has purposed for our lives.

The church is to be a witness, a testimony of God's very existence, His glory, power, and love. Jesus' life clearly did that. He glorified the Father. When humankind saw Jesus, the Father was revealed through Him. Jesus explained how He glorified God: He finished the work the Father gave Him to do.

To glorify God is to faithfully complete an assignment, to do those things He has called, chosen, appointed, and anointed us to do.[76]

Just as the Code Talkers were appointed to complete their assignment, they finished the work according to their instructions by using the code.

It is the same way with natural things. When something is to be built, it must be done according to the design instructions and it must comply with the building code. The Kingdom is at hand and we have to build according to the heavenly code of God's Word communicated to us by the Holy Spirit. Otherwise, it will not stand.

Because the Navajo Code Talkers knew their end could come at any time, they were serious and watchful in their prayers. They succeeded and were victorious in battle because they followed the instructions of the code.

---

[75] Matthew 4:17
[76] John 17:4-26

"But the end of all things is at hand; therefore be serious and watchful in your prayers."

— 1 Peter 4:7

The battle was won according to the code.

Now, then, the question is: Are you building your spiritual life and the Kingdom of God according to the Code of the Spirit?

A Prayer for Fallen Warriors

There is a burden in me to pray for the prayer warriors and intercessors that have fallen away from the divinely appointed role for their lives.

The fulfilled calling of the true intercessor makes a great difference in the spirit realm. Thus, they in-turn make a huge difference in our nation.

Many warriors/intercessors have been wounded and hurt. In this they have been sidetracked from their Godly place of power and influence. Prayer warrior, it is your time to once again posture yourself by standing in your appointed place in these great and mighty last days before the coming of the Lord!

You can make a difference!
You are the difference!

Agree with me today and pray:

Father in Heaven, I come to you to ask forgiveness for my sins. Creator, saturate me with your cleansing and healing blood right now. Help me to lay down every hurt and wound I have been carrying. I release them now and give them to You. I refuse to hold on to anything that holds me back from my assigned place in the spirit.

I receive and put on all the armor you have provided for me. I lift up my sword of Your Word as I march forward this day into the great and mighty plan you have for me and our nation.

Thank you.
I love you Creator God, in Jesus name.
Amen.

> So I sought for a man among them who would make a wall, and stand in the gap before Me on behalf of the land, that I should not destroy it; but I found no one.
>
> Ezekiel 22:30

Contact the author at:
Abundant Living Fellowship
(760) 252-5446
alfmatt610@yahoo.com